Child-rearing has never been an easy assignment. And today it is harder than ever. The world seems to be spinning faster. An avalanche of new knowledge comes crashing in.

Children are growing up under much different circumstances than parents experienced. The new generation faces more competition, more powerful peer-group pressures, and immense emotional stress.

This means that good parents are needed more than ever. It means that building lives takes time, tolerance, patience, faith, self-sacrifice, love, and work.

But nothing is more rewarding than watching a child move into maturity and independence. We will never have a greater opportunity than helping children become persons who accept responsibility and right living.

In sensing the large task of rearing children, we may be immobilized by fear or empowered by faith. We may be overcome by the perils and problems or challenged by the possibilities and potential.

This small volume discusses seven of the most basic needs of the growing child (and of all of us throughout life).

Seven Things Children Need

John M. Drescher

**Introduction by
Evelyn and Sylvanus Duvall**

HERALD PRESS
Scottdale, Pennsylvania
Kitchener, Ontario

Scripture quotations, unless otherwise indicated, are used by permission from the Revised Standard Version, Old Testament Section, Copyright 1952; New Testament Section, First Edition, Copyright 1946; New Testament Section, Second Edition, © 1971 by Division of Christian Education of the National Council of the Churches of Christ in the U.S.A.

Verses marked "Phillips" are from *The New Testament in Modern English*, Revised Edition, © J. B. Phillips, 1958, 1960, 1972. By permission of Macmillan Publishing Co., Inc., and William Collins Sons & Co, Ltd.

Excerpts from *The Jerusalem Bible*, © 1966 by Darton, Longman & Todd, Ltd. and Doubleday & Company, Inc. Used by permission of the publisher.

The poem at the beginning of chapter 1 is reprinted from *The Prophet*, by Khalil Gibran, with permission of the publisher, Alfred A. Knopf, Inc. Copyright 1923 by Khalil Gibran; renewal copyright 1951 by Administrators C.T.A. of Khalil Gibran Estate and Mary G. Gibran.

To the group of parents
from Scottdale Mennonite Church,
Scottdale, Pennsylvania, who encouraged
publication of these chapters following a
retreat at Laurelville Church Center,
Mt. Pleasant, Pennsylvania, where the
basic content of this book was shared
and discussed.

CONTENTS

AUTHOR'S PREFACE

Dave handed his dad his report card. While his father stood silent, still in a state of shock, Dave asked, "Dad, do you think those grades are the result of heredity or environment?"

Many parents today are not sure whether the problems of their children are the result of what they inherited or learned from their parents, or of pressures and patterns produced by society.

North American parents lead the world in buying books on child care. Yet many parents feel helpless and wonder what or who is responsible for their child's behavior.

Child-rearing has never been an easy assignment. And today it is harder than ever. The world seems to be spinning faster. An avalanche of new knowledge comes crashing in. Children are growing up under much different circumstances than parents experienced. The new generation faces more competition, more powerful peer-group pressures, and immense emotional stress.

This means that good parents are needed more than ever. It means that building lives takes time, tolerance, patience, faith, self-sacrifice, love, and work. But nothing is more rewarding than watching a child move into maturity and independence. We will never have a greater opportunity than helping children become persons who accept responsibility and right living.

In sensing the large task of rearing children, we may be immobilized by fear or empowered by faith. We may be overcome by the perils and problems or challenged by the possibilities and potential.

We are told by psychologists, by study, by common sense, and by an understanding of ourselves that each child has certain basic needs. Adults also have the same needs, regardless of age. Yet the chapters which follow point out that the meeting of these needs is of a paramount importance in the early years when attitudes and approaches to life are molded. If these needs are not met early, the child will be disturbed and seek fulfillment in wrong and many times hurtful ways.

Psychiatrist Karl Menninger says we move in one of two directions if basic needs are not met. We withdraw and turn in upon ourselves, which he describes as a *flight* reaction. Or we develop the *fight* reaction and become aggressors, turning against others.

This small volume discusses seven of the most basic needs of the growing child (and of all of us throughout life).

What is shared in these chapters began as ten-minute talks preceding more lengthy discussions on varied subjects. Over the years each has been added to through reading, sharing in retreats, and additional observations. The more formal and final form of these chapters developed following a retreat with thirty parents where the ideas were discussed and debated.

I am indebted to a large array of persons, books, and articles; some are listed in the bibliography, but many I no longer recall.

An earnest effort was made to write a practical, personal, down-to-earth book which might provide a resource for families, discussion groups, church classes, school groups, family retreats, and the like. Numerous subheadings are used for easy reading and reference. A quiz and discussion questions at the end of each chapter are included as stimuli for discussion.

This book goes forth with the earnest prayer that it will help many parents in the hard but happy responsibility of better meeting the basic needs of their children.

John M. Drescher
Scottdale, Pennsylvania

INTRODUCTION

We have worked for many years as a professional team, as well as being actively practicing parents and grandparents. So when *Seven Things Children Need* arrived, we both read it, talked it over, and shared in writing this introduction.

This book is a joy to read, and we predict that many a parent will profit by it. The author is familiar with the basic concepts of child development. These he has sifted to bring the reader the gist of what is generally accepted, without cumbersome ifs, ands, or buts.

The treatment given the needs of children is in emotional and spiritual terms. In an age when needs are seen so often in terms of things, this is a welcome emphasis.

Sources of authority are well balanced. The author clearly sees parents, poets, practical persons of experience such as judges, as well as the experts in child development as having insights into the needs of children. He generously shares his own rich personal experience in ways that are helpful.

Each of the chapter topics is woven throughout the entire book. Discipline, for instance, is one chapter, as well as the focus of other subjects where it is relevant.

Although the book is concerned primarily with children, it is not so much child-centered as person-centered. Children are seen as part of the larger constellation of the family in its world.

Considerable use of anecdotal material makes the reader feel, "He had me in mind!" Perhaps this is one worthy result of the material's having been worked through with groups of parents so that it is realistic and does not demand too much of them.

John Drescher quite evidently expects his readers to talk back to him. After each chapter there are quizzes and subjects for further discussion. The appendix has a still larger quiz on permissiveness that is a welcome addition.

Readers who take full advantage of opportunities to discuss and react to what the author says will get most from this book. You may want to go beyond merely answering the questions that are posed and to ask some of your own. For instance:

Is the author expecting too much of parents? Not enough?

Does parenthood have to be a burdensome responsibility?

What about the joy that children bring their parents?

How would I define the challenge of parenthood?

Herald Press is to be congratulated in publishing so worthy and helpful a book concerned with the most basic question of human society — the quality of our children.

Evelyn M. Duvall, PhD
Sylvanus M. Duvall, PhD
Sarasota, Florida

1
The Need for Significance

And a woman who held a babe against
her bosom said, Speak to us of Children.
　And he said:
　Your children are not your children.
　They are the sons and daughters of Life's
longing for itself.
　They come through you but not from
you,
　And though they are with you yet they
belong not to you.

　You may give them your love but not
your thoughts,
　For they have their own thoughts,
　You may house their bodies but not
their souls,
　For their souls dwell in the house of to-
morrow, which you cannot visit, not even
in your dreams.
　You may strive to be like them, but seek
not to make them like you.
　For life goes not backward nor tarries
with yesterday.
　You are the bows from which your children as living arrows are sent forth.
　The archer sees the mark upon the path
of the infinite, and He bends you with His
might that His arrows may go swift and far.

Let your bending in the archer's hand
be for gladness;
For even as He loves the arrow that flies,
so He loves also the bow that is stable.
— From *The Prophet,* by Khalil Gibran

∘   ∘   ∘

When someone is deprived of his self-esteem,
he is deprived of the one thing that makes a
person worth loving. For one's own benefit, if
for no other reason, the effort should be to build
self-esteem in the other, to confirm rather than
to assault it. This is achieved, not by flattery,
but by a generous appreciation of the other's
strengths and a generous deemphasis of his
weaknesses, by speaking of his good points and
as rarely as possible about his bad ones. People who are good to each other make each other
good. — Jo Coudert

CHILDREN NEED A
SENSE OF SIGNIFICANCE

THREE preschoolers were at play. For a time they interacted with a great deal of common interest and enthusiasm. Then two went off and played by themselves, ignoring the third playmate. Before long the lone one cried out, "I'm here! I'm here! Don't you see I'm here?"

Although the little boy could not philosophize about his response or analyze it psychologically or phrase it theologically, he expressed a need which is universal. He wanted to be noticed and recognized as a person of worth.

A healthy sense of personal worth is essential. It is almost impossible to live with ourselves if we feel we are of little value or if we don't like ourselves. A person who feels like a nobody will contribute little to life. This needs to be stressed here because the great plague of inferiority feelings starts early in life. We human beings need to be noticed, appreciated, and loved as we are, if we are to have a sense of significance.

One day a group of first-graders were shown through a dairy. At the end of the tour the leader asked, "Are there any questions?" A small hand went up. "Did you see my new sweater?" So the small child seeks attention. If not noticed in proper conduct, the child may seek it by spilling milk, throwing things on the floor, or in destructive ways. As someone suggested, "A spanking is preferred to being ignored."

A child may not eat properly because he has learned that if he stalls his parents will make a great fuss over him. He enjoys attention. Ignore his delaying tactics and before long he will eat normally again. One child may throw tantrums and upset games to force himself to the center of the scene. Another may yell and scream at appropriate places and persons to get attention.

If such behavior ended with childhood, perhaps we could endure it and not worry about those few short years. But the youth, who has not gained a proper sense of significance, races his car, lays rubber on the highway, draws attention by loudness in speech or dress, or in a dozen other ways demands notice.

Adults also call attention to themselves and desire to be recognized as persons, but often in more subtle ways, such as displaying something they have made or describing somewhere they have been. Grown people will dominate the conversation, dress flamboyantly, demand leadership or office, or strive like fools for an honor or degree, deserved or undeserved.

But how can this basic need for significance be met in the life of a child? Sometimes we start with wrong assumptions.

Three False Assumptions

The first false assumption is that the parent-child relationship should take priority over the husband-wife relationship. Dr. Alfred A. Nesser, of Emory University School of Medicine, warns against child-oriented homes. "Perhaps the most significant element in the dissolution of long-standing marriages is a consequence of living in the century of the child," he says.

Parent-child relationships have been stressed so strongly for several decades that, for the sake of the child, husband-wife priorities are many times laid aside too easily. After the first child comes, a real test takes place. Will the mother rob her husband of time and love for the sake of the child and hinder that relationship or will she continue to give her husband top priority? As one husband notes, "I had a fine wife until our first child was born. Then Mary became more mother than mate."

It is good to recall that marriage is permanent while parenthood is passing. Since marriage begins and ends with two persons, the primary concern is to keep the relationship in the best possible repair. When this is the case, the child relationship tends to take care of itself rather well. Louis M. Terman writes, "If a wife does not love her husband more than she loves her children, both the children and the marriage are in danger." When a husband is assured that his wife's love has not diminished, he is usually more than willing to help care for the child and do his share of household chores.

Nothing is so central for a child's happiness and sense of worth as the love of father and mother for each other. There is no better way of giving the child a sense of significance than to allow him to see and to feel the closeness and commitment of his mother and father.

Parents should spend more time and effort developing their own personalities and relationships. If father and mother are happy with each other, that contentment is conveyed to the child. This results not only in good behavior and affection, but in a sense of personal worth.

Parents should show affection and love for each other in front of the children. The husband should call his wife by her name, not "Mother." Leave "Mother" for the children. "The lack of affection between father and mother is the greatest cause of delinquency I know," says Judge Philip Gilliam.

Parents should spend extra time and effort cultivating their friendship as husband and wife. When parents enrich their lives together, they are at the same time enriching their children's lives and the children can feel it.

A *second false assumption is that the child rightfully deserves to be the center of attention*. Too often everything is bent for the child's benefit or wishes. The result is that we develop self-centered children. If they do not receive what they want, they are likely to react, rebel, or run away. "What can I get?" rather

22

than "What can I give?" becomes a way of life.

Jean Laird writes: "Most of us want our children's love more than anything else, and feel it represents proof that we are doing a good job of being parents. In former years, the majority of parents wanted mainly respect from their children, which made things considerably easier. They weren't afraid to be momentarily disliked by children during the act of enforcing rules.

"Now a psychological revolution is taking place in our homes. Parents feel weighed down with a sense of guilty responsibility. They have been made acutely aware of the complex emotional relationship between parent and child and are thinking in terms of psychological cause and effect. We parents are led to believe that everything we say and do to our children will have a lasting effect for good or evil.

"As a result, many of us have become uneasy, embarrassed, inarticulate, and frightened — the first generation of immobilized parents who are letting their children practically take over their homes." Children are not meant to be the center of the family. The rightful center is the relationship of husband and wife.

A third false assumption is that the child should be pushed as rapidly as possible into more mature roles. We have an awful problem letting children be children — so we do ridiculous things. At three months we select toys parents like to play with. Three-year-olds receive electric trains. Many a tricycle stands for months awaiting a driver still in diapers. We dress five-year-olds in caps and gowns for kindergarten graduation. One little fellow said, "I think it's bad that I graduated and can't even read."

Little girls who would like to play with dolls are driven downtown to learn to dance. We frustrate tots by pairing them off in first grade, electing them to class offices, and putting them on committees before they know what it means. We dress them like adults. In baseball we expect them to perform as professionals before they have hips big enough to hold up their uniforms or hands big enough to grasp the ball. We push them to read while they still prefer to stack blocks.

Why? Because many parents seek vicarious fulfillment in their children. They want their children to experience and achieve things they themselves were denied. Their children become their ego trip. By forcing their children into premature roles, they build feelings of frustration and incompetence.

The three main areas where Americans and Canadians are expected to excel are in beauty, intelligence, and possessions. A child constantly pressured to measure up, to be superior, to excel in these things rather than being himself, will suffer for it. Inferiority feelings, which arise out of the great drive for superiority, grow by leaps and bounds.

Destructive Forces

One man remembers vividly that when visitors came to his home during his childhood his parents often showed photographs of his older brother. "Look what a lovely baby he was," they would exclaim about his brother. But no photographs were ever shown of him. His brother always seemed to do everything right and was clever and neat in his appearance, whereas he always seemed to be in trouble. The younger brother felt his parents looked for him only if something was broken. One night they found him sobbing in the attic, feeling no one loved him at all. To wound the self-respect of a little child in this way is to hurt him far more than a whipping, and to scar him for life.

A father said to his son, "I don't know what you're going to be. I can't imagine anybody giving you a job. You'll never make anything of life." If a child is told often enough that he will never amount to anything, he will begin to believe it. If he doesn't turn out well, it will not be his own fault entirely. A large share of the responsibility must be laid at the door of a parent, who in robbing a child of his self-respect, robs him of a God-given quality which is one of the greatest driving forces of personality.

In the same way, ridicule, sarcasm, scorn, and contempt directed at a child produce feelings of inferiority and should be avoided. In a parent's fit of anger, a child's mind may be injured and his emotions scarred. If repressed or bottled up, these feelings may produce neurotic symptoms which can result in serious emotional problems later in life.

Even to laugh at a child who mispronounces a word or makes some error may drive him to dishonesty and lying to protect his self-respect.

25

How Build a Sense of Significance?

Now we come to the positive.

1. *Your attitude as a parent toward yourself is basic and will affect your child's self-esteem.* If you as a parent have a sense of worth, you will convey a sense of worth to your child.

2. *Let your child help around the home.* To grow is to be needed. "Let me do it" begins early. The temptation is to turn the child away and do it oneself. But the small child loves to help and needs meaningful experiences if he is to learn responsibility. How else will a child learn to make cookies, paint the fence, or hammer nails?

To compliment the child early when he does small jobs gives a sense of significance. Later, daily chores give a sense of regular accomplishment. Bruno Bettelheim writes, "Conviction about one's worth comes only from feeling that one has important tasks and . has met them well." So let the child help. Avoid the painful phrase, "Oh, you can't do that."

3. *Introduce your child to others.* An editor friend of mine traveled across North America in the interests of a youth magazine. He told me he could predict the climate of relationships between youth and their parents almost every time by noticing if the parents introduced their children to him by name. One's name is awfully important to a child as well as an adult. When parents or others think a child worthy of introduction by name, it helps contribute to his developing sense of worth.

4. *Let the child speak for himself.* We often humiliate a child by answering for him. It is

rude for parents to respond to a question asked of a child. I've even heard college students asked, "How is college going?" and a parent respond, "Oh, she's doing fine — she's on the dean's list," or "He made the football team."

In a group of youth counselors, the concern was expressed that when a youth is brought in for an interview, the parents frequently do the talking. No doubt that's a large part of the problem.

Why do parents speak for a child, undermining his self-respect and subtracting from his significance? Because parents do not respect the child as a person and want to assert their own importance. In so doing they signal the child that he is insignificant and not qualified to speak for himself.

5. *Give the child the privilege of choice and respect his opinions whenever possible*. Personality develops through making decisions. Children should be given many opportunities to choose, and should learn to live with the results of their decisions.

Certain matters demand the decision of parents, of course. But many choices have no ethical or eternal significance. When we allow children to choose we give them a sense of worth.

6. *Spend time with your child*. If parents do not take time for their children, children will take time from them in unpleasant ways such as whining, fighting, and other angry behavior patterns.

A small boy watched his father polish the car. He asked, "Dad, your car's worth a lot, isn't it?"

"Yes," his dad replied, "it cost a lot. It pays to take care of it. When I trade the car in, it will be worth more if I take care of it."

After some silence the son said, "Dad, I guess I'm not worth very much, am I?"

We build a child's sense of self-worth when we take time to listen to his concerns, when we drop the newspaper when he speaks, when we look into his eyes when he shares with us.

Another boy came to his father who was reading the paper. He tried to show him a scratch on his hand. Annoyed by the interruption, his dad, still looking at the paper, said, "Well, I can't do anything about it, can I?"

The small one replied, "Yes, Daddy, you could have said, 'Oh.' "

A mother shared how her small son came to her over a two-day period complaining a number of times that he had a blister on his hand. Each time she said, "You'll have to take care not to hurt yourself." But she didn't look at his hand. Before leaving him with a babysitter to attend a retreat on parent-child problems, she finally stopped to look at his hand. She saw that it needed immediate attention because a splinter was causing infection. She wished then that she had taken time earlier to take her son's problem seriously.

7. *Encourage the feeling of worth and significance by trusting your child occasionally with things which surprise him.* Some time ago my sister and family came to visit us. "Where is Jerry?" we all wanted to know. Fourteen-year-old Jerry was not with them. His dad replied,

"We left him at home to attend a sale and bid on a farm tractor." We were startled at the idea. But Jerry's parents seemed perfectly relaxed. And what a feeling of worth Jerry must have had!

One family put both teenage sons, ages thirteen and fifteen, on their joint checking account. "Why not?" the father asked. "Should I trust Wall Street more than my own sons?"

Children grow in responsibility and accomplishment as they are trusted. And to trust them at times with things which surprise them can give them a big boost toward the sense of worth which is so basic to all of life.

Dorothy Briggs concludes in *Your Child and Self-Esteem: The Key to His Life*, after twenty-six years of clinical work, "What's the greatest gift you can give your child? Help him to like himself."

SIGNIFICANCE QUIZ FOR PARENTS

Check the answer in the appropriate column: true, false, or usually.

T   F   U

—— —— —— 1. spend some time with my child personally each day I'm home.

—— —— —— 2. I give my child special responsibilities to prove I trust him.

—— —— —— 3. I try not to force my child into roles for which he is unready.

—— —— —— 4. I introduce my children to visitors by name.

— — — 5. I believe our husband-wife relationship takes priority over our parent-child relationship.

— — — 6. As parents, we show affection for each other in front of our children.

— — — 7. I allow the children to help do things.

FOR DISCUSSION

1. Discuss times you remember when parent-child relationships took priority over husband-wife relationships.

2. How free should parents be to show affection in front of their children?

3. Give examples from your own experience when you forced children into roles for which they were not ready.

4. Discuss the statement, "Inferiority feelings grow out of the drive for superiority."

5. Do you think you are ever justified in answering for your child?

6. What are some things you might trust your child with to surprise him and show confidence in him?

7. What are some ways children of different ages assert themselves to bolster their sense of significance?

8. Discuss Gibran's poem at the beginning of this chapter. Where do you agree or disagree?

9. If possible read *Hide or Seek*, by James Dobson, published by Revell.

2
The Need for
Security

Parents cannot change the color of their child's eyes, but they can give to eyes the light of understanding's warmth of sympathy. They cannot much alter the child's features, but they can in many ways endow the child with the glow of humaneness, kindness, and friendliness, which may in the long run bring a lot more happiness than the perfection that wins beauty contests. Parents cannot give security by surrounding the child with an abundance of things but enclosing the child in the arms of love.

* * *

Overpossessive and overpermissive parents build insecurity into the life of their children. "Love that possesses," says Peter Bertocci, "is love that destroys more than it creates." The child needs a context to develop into a person — a strong selfhood, useful and true. When the parent is too possessive, the child's personality is dwarfed as surely as a seedling which springs up too close to a full-grown tree. The overpossessive parent loves the child primarily for what the child does for the parent. This is a hurtful, selfish love.

On the other hand, the overpermissive parent who furnishes no clear restrictions or walls will rear a child who feels ill-at-ease. Though rules should be few, yet those few rules consistently held build stability.

There are two freedoms: the false where one is free to do what he likes, and the true where he is free to do what he ought. — Charles Kingsley

CHILDREN
NEED SECURITY

JIM CAME for counsel of his own accord. At nineteen he was an example of incapacitating insecurity. Several sessions revealed many reasons for this. He said he never knew a happy day in his life. Although he tried to put on a big front, inside he was always running away, afraid. He turned to drugs and alcohol to prop up his life and keep him going. Now he was at the end of his rope. In desperation he sought help.

A child craves security. He may cling to a security blanket, or drag a teddy bear or rag doll with him wherever he goes. The child has an inner need to be certain, to be safe, to have solid ground under his feet. He experiences fear when the familiar is not present. Healy and Bronner in *New Light on Delinquency and Its Treatment* say that if a child's basic need for security is not met, he will be robbing candy stores by the time he is eight.

Conditions Which Create Insecurity

Not all the reasons for insecurity are portrayed in the experience of Jim, but some major ones are present. What are they?

1. Parental conflict. Jim never knew the time when his parents lived in love and peace. They were constantly quarreling. There was tension. He was caught in the middle. He felt at any time his family might fly apart.

In one study of troubled teenagers the three most frequently mentioned reasons for using drugs (in order of times mentioned) were: (1) parental conflict, (2) desire for personality change, and (3) peer group pressure. The teen-agers had parents who were continually fighting; they didn't like themselves and wanted to change their personalities through drugs; and they yielded to the use of drugs because of the pressure they felt from others.

Few things are more threatening to a child than to see those he knows best, on whom his life depends, as antagonists who are continually quarreling. This does not mean parents should never argue in front of their children. To have sharp differences and to resolve them in love can help the child face life realistically. If he observes love between his parents following a disagreement, he is probably better equipped to meet conflict himself than the child who never knew his parents had differences. This, however, is in contrast to parents who continually fight.

2. *Mobility*. Jim's family had moved again and again. Jim never felt at home anywhere. He never developed close friendships, and he dreaded the thought of new situations.

Many of today's families are continually on the move. More than one fourth the population moves each year. Few families stay at the same house for ten or more years. The strengthening and stablizing forces of the extended family are frequently missing for both parents and children.

Several years ago a small son seemed sick. Repeated examinations by a medical doctor failed to reveal any reasons for the illness. After many months the boy confessed to his parents, "I was afraid you would move again while I was at school."

Moving to a new community forces a child to adjust to new friends, a new school, a new house, and many other new experiences. Such a child can easily develop feelings of insecurity, especially if he does not enjoy the warmth and strength of deep love relationships with brothers, sisters, and parents.

3. *Lack of proper discipline*. Jim never knew where the real boundaries were for his life. When his parents felt good, they were overpermissive. When they were at odds about anything, Jim was the easiest target on which to vent their hostilities.

To enjoy security and a sense of well-being, a child needs some rules for life. The most insecure children come from homes where there are no clear boundaries for their behavior. Some teenagers complain that their parents do not care enough for them to set such boundaries. Young people may act as if they are abused or treated unfairly when limits are set, yet they are secretly pleased because the limits give them a sense of security. Mother and Father care.

Discipline as a basic need will be discussed in a later chapter. But since it has so much to do with a sense of security it is mentioned briefly here.

A seventeen-year-old girl found it difficult to believe that God loved her, because she could no longer believe in human love. She was miserable. In admitting this to her counselor, she disclosed that love was poorly communicated at home. She never really knew for sure that she was loved or even wanted.

One day at a friend's house, she saw the mother kiss the girl good-by and say, "Now dear, I expect you to be home tonight at eleven o'clock. Don't be late. I'll be waiting for you." Like a stab through her heart, she wondered why her own mother never seemed to care where she was or when she came home. To find out if her family really cared for her, she decided to stay out so late that they would be frightened about her welfare or perhaps call the police.

She went to a late show just to have a place to sit. Then she walked the streets alone until she became afraid. She went to a depot and slouched on a bench, desperately tired and longing for bed, but determined to get her answer.

As dawn broke she finally stumbled up to the front door of her home, purposely entering noisily in the hope that someone would hear. No one called out; no one paid any attention. At breakfast no one asked where she was during the night, or when she came home. She had her answer! With this deep hurt in her heart she was dragging herself through life.

4. Absence of parents. Jim not only experienced the newness of one community after another, but his parents were often absent. Dad was seldom home, even evenings. Because his mother had a job, Jim came home from school each afternoon to an empty house. Absence of parents builds insecurity.

A research student phoned a dozen homes around nine o'clock in the evening to see if parents knew where their children were. "My first five calls were answered by children who had no idea where their parents were," he reported.

5. Continual criticism. Jim's parents heaped constant criticism on him. He felt that nothing he did was ever right. A terrible fear of failure was always present. He lived with a deep sense of incompetence. In applying for a job, his insecurity always came through to the interviewer. In tackling a new task he was sure he could not succeed. He felt rejected.

Sheldon and Eleanor Glueck, in *The Making of a Delinquent, One Thousand Juvenile Delinquents,* and similar studies, show that rejection by parents is a major factor leading children to a life of crime.

A child is crushed if he feels his parents do not like him, constantly criticize him, and do not have time for him, or if he senses they did not want him in the first place. A parent can also cause feelings of rejection by doing things for the child with an air of martyrdom.

6. *Things rather than persons.* Jim had the distinct feeling that his parents constantly gave him things and money rather than themselves. On his birthday and at Christmas they showered him with gifts. But even as a young child he wanted *them* rather than their gifts. As he became older, it seemed to Jim that his parents' money and gifts were guilt payment to him for their lack of time and love.

The lyrics of a number of songs during the past few decades tell of parents who gave everything but themselves. Many of these were written by insecure, alienated young people.

7. *Insecure parents.* Back of the insecurity of youth, though, is the fact that many parents themselves feel insecure. The unstable world situation takes its toll. An eight-year-old boy, whose family moved into a beautiful new home in the city, seemed anxious and worried. When his parents finally persuaded him to admit what was troubling him, he said that he wished they had moved to the country because the city might be bombed. He had heard his parents talking about the threat of nuclear war which would likely wipe out major cities.

Talk of the spiraling cost of living, rising taxes, a new economic depression, crop failure, natural disasters, war, job insecurity, and a multitude of other problems, discussed carelessly in front of children can cause 'fear and insecurity. Parents who also discuss in the presence of their children the problems of delinquency, drugs, sex, and their own insecurities about rearing a family can cause inner panic. One little child who overheard his parents talking about pollution asked, "Mother, are you sure there will be enough air for everyone?"

Ours is an age of anxiety. It is an age when children attempt to shoulder to a greater degree than they should the worries of their parents.

Insecure parents usually have great difficulty providing consistent discipline. They shift from one extreme to another. They move from permissiveness with their children to severity, depending on the mood of the moment. When they take a firm stand on anything they feel they are probably wrong in being so strict. When they fail to assert what they down deep know to be right, they feel guilty.

A child soon learns to play insecure parents against each other. He uses their insecurity to achieve his immediate desires which are often ultimately harmful. The child, to be secure, needs to know where he stands. When he realizes that his parents' expectations are built on shifting sand, he feels insecure.

What Builds Security?

One could simply say that changing all the above comments from negative to positive statements would reveal how to provide a child with the security he needs. This is correct. But let's look more closely at seven positive factors in building a child's sense of security.

1. Security between father and mother. The

love which father and mother have for each other is the most important of these. Constant bickering between parents tears a child apart and leaves him no ground on which to stand. Beneath the surface of occasional differences of opinion, the child should always be able to sense love, trust, and loyalty.

Considering the large number of desertions and divorces, no wonder so many children are insecure. A man writes of his childhood, "I never witnessed a kiss between my parents. My chief difficulty as a child was a terrifying sense of insecurity." Speaking of mother and father relationships Dr. David Goodman says, "Your baby will smile at you and later at the world, if you two never cease to smile at each other. No fact of child training is truer or more important than this."

Dr. Kenneth Foreman writes, "The probation officer of Louisville, Kentucky, has said that delinquent children come from all sorts of homes but one. He has never found a delinquent child with the background of a home where harmony reigned between husband and wife." Psychiatrist Justin S. Green agrees. "In my twenty-five years of practice, I have yet to see a serious emotional problem in a child whose parents loved each other, and whose love for the child was an outgrowth of their love."

2. *A rich and continuing love of parents for child.* Through the parents' loving care, the child acquires his first sense of being safe in a strange new world. This abiding love means acceptance when the child is good or bad. A child is ex-

tremely sensitive to not being wanted. To feel secure a child needs to be held, hugged, and told he is loved. Love helps a child face whatever comes.

A little fellow suffering in the hospital was complimented on the way he was taking it. "You can stand almost anything when you know your folks love you," he replied. When a child is secure in the love of his family he can take the ridicule of peers. He can stand up to the pressure of "Everybody is doing it." He can keep his head up when he loses a game or an election at school. He can face whatever comes.

A doctor asked a young girl, "What does home mean to you?" She replied, "Home is the place you go when it gets dark." A child who can return to the security of a loving home when it gets dark is blessed indeed. How sad that for many children home is also dark.

3. *Family togetherness.* A child feels a sense of stability and security when he experiences strong family unity. Author Gordon in *A Touch of Wonder* tells of many things his family did together when he was a boy. "No doubt in my childhood I had the usual quota of playthings, but these are forgotten now. What I remember," he recalls with pleasure, "is the day we rode in a caboose, the time we tried to skin the alligator, the telegraph we made that really worked. I remember the trophy table in the hall where we children were encouraged to exhibit things we had found — snakeskins, seashells, flowers, arrowheads — anything unusual or beautiful."

Studies show that children start running with

the wrong crowd when they lack a feeling of togetherness in the family. In rehabilitating children who lost both parents in World War II, it was found that those who remembered doing many things together as a family were best able to achieve a new sense of normalcy.

In a retreat group on the family, a Swiss woman shared her experience. In her childhood her family had few material things. Love was seldom openly known. But a memory she cherishes above all others is the day her mother took off an entire afternoon to make her a straw doll. That simple act did for her what no amount of money could do.

A kindergarten teacher from our town asked her class before Mother's Day, "Why do you think your mother is the greatest?" Their answers were revealing. Note the types of responses that predominate. Little things done together stand out. It would be interesting also to analyze what is absent from the list. Here is the list:

1. My mother plays with me a lot.
2. Because she played Bingo last night and she gave me medicine for my cold.
3. Because she buys me stuff.
4. Because my mother washes clothes for us and kisses me good-bye when I go to school.
5. Because she cooks, washes clothes, and loves me.
6. Because she cooks dinner for me and mows the grass.
7. Because she cooks for us.
8. Because she bakes potatoes and fixes supper, and takes care of my baby brother.
9. I can't think of any words. (This could mean a lot.)

44

10. Because she hugs me and she is so-o-o-o beautiful.
11. Because she kisses and hugs me and takes care of me.
12. She is the best cook and fixes me a bowl of soup.
13. She cooks my food and puts me to bed.
14. She cooks my dad's steak.
15. She cleans the house, makes the beds, and washes the dishes so we can eat all the time.
16. Because she makes treats for my birthday.
17. Because she makes our beds and covers us up at night.
18. Because she helps me, Jeff, Greg, and Dad play Ping-Pong.
19. Because she helps us do things. She makes food and calls us when it's suppertime.
20. Because I love her, and my dad loves her a lot, and my brother doesn't like to kiss her, but once my grandmother kissed him when he was sleeping. Ha!
21. I don't know why.
22. Because she makes popcorn and she's always nice to me.
23. Because she gives me all the medicine I need and takes care of me.

A good bit of security is scattered through these statements.

4. Regular routine. Regular times for doing things in the family builds security. This does not mean iron-clad rules that can never be changed. What it does mean is that a usual schedule for meals, family chores, and going to bed is good and builds healthy relationships.

5. Proper discipline. Overpermissive, indecisive parents who leave a child to the mercy of every passing whim or impulse are a real threat to a child's security. The child never knows clearly what is expected of him or what he may or may not do. Discipline, administered fairly and in love, brings peace and order into a child's life.

6. *Touching your child.* Recently considerable attention has been given to what touching others does in building security and acceptance. Dr. Frederic Burke, a pediatrician in Washington, D.C., points out the importance of father and mother rocking their baby. "I strongly recommend a rocker," he says. "And here at Georgetown University we practice what we preach. We have put rocking chairs in all our nurseries. They help both mother and the child.

"Most young mothers realize that an infant needs handling, stroking, coddling, and cooing," Dr. Burke continues. "All these things are pleasant and soft and reinforcing to the security of the infant. . . . I firmly believe that early physical experience with parents' loving hands and arms is imprinted in the child's mind; and while apparently forgotten, it has a tremendous influence on the child's ego and the kind of adolescent he or she becomes."

So touch, skin to skin, is rightly stressed today as an important part of a child's experience. Breast-feeding is recommended if at all possible. Holding the child frequently and touching him when speaking to him are positive psychological forces in building inner security, satisfaction, and strong relationships. We communicate a great deal by touch. Some people have great difficulty in getting close to others as adults and in functioning well in marriage because they were never physically close to their parents.

Holding the child, placing a hand on his shoulder, hugging and kissing him, and grasping his hand while walking — all these help create a closeness and a solid relationship. This feeling cannot be replaced by lavishing on a child the things money can buy.

7. *A sense of belonging.* Belonging is a deep psychological need. A child wants to be a part of a family, a class, or a team. If he senses he doesn't belong, he is sure to feel insecure.

"Some years ago the *New York Times* printed a human-interest story entitled 'He Would Like to Belong.' The article told about a small boy who was riding on a downtown bus. There he sat, huddled close to a lady in a gray suit. Naturally everyone thought he belonged to her. Little wonder, then, that when he rubbed his dirty shoes against a woman sitting on the other side of him, she said to the lady in the gray suit, 'Pardon me, but would you please make your little boy take his feet off the seat? His shoes are getting my dress dirty.'

"The woman in gray blushed. Then giving the boy a little shove, she said, 'He's not my boy. I never saw him before.'

"The lad squirmed uneasily. He was such a tiny little fellow, his feet dangling off the seat. He lowered his eyes and tried desperately to hold back a sob.

" 'I'm sorry I got your dress dirty,' he said to the woman, 'I didn't mean to?'

" 'Oh, that's all right,' she answered, a little embarrassed. Then, since his eyes were still fastened upon her, she added, 'Are you going somewhere — alone?'

" 'Yes,' he nodded, 'I always go alone. There isn't anyone to go with me. I don't have any mommy or daddy. They're both dead. I live with Aunt Clara but she says Aunt Mildred ought to help take care of me part of the time. So when she gets tired of me and wants to go someplace, she sends me over to stay with Aunt Mildred.'

" 'Oh,' said the woman, 'are you on your way to Aunt Mildred's now?'

" 'Yes,' the boy continued, 'but sometimes Aunt Mildred isn't home. I sure hope she's there today because it looks like it's gonna rain and I don't want to be out in the street when it rains.'

"The woman felt a little lump in her throat as she said, 'You're a very little boy to be shifted around like this.'

" 'Oh, I don't mind,' he said. 'I never get lost. But I get lonesome sometimes. So when I see someone that I think I would like to belong to, I sit real close and snuggle up and pretend I really do belong to them. I was playing that I belonged to this other lady when I got your dress dirty. I forgot about my feet.'

"The woman put her arms around the little fellow and snuggled him up so close that it almost hurt. He wanted to belong to someone. And deep in her heart she wished that he belonged to her.

"This little boy, in his artless, childlike fashion, had expressed a universal need. And it doesn't matter who he is or how old he is: everyone wants to belong."*

A sense of belonging is essential for a child's security and feeling of worth. And when a child feels he belongs in his family and is of real worth there, it is not a big step also to feel accepted, loved, and of worth to others and to God.

A man whose father was well known remembers how, as a little boy, he missed his daddy

---

*Clyde M. Narramore, *This Way to Happiness* (Grand Rapids: Zondervan, 1962), pp. 54-55.

when public engagements took him away a great deal. One night, when his father was expected home, the boy wanted to wait up to greet his father. However, he was sent to bed, for misbehaving. He awoke between ten and eleven and heard his father's voice. He got up, dressed, and came downstairs. He simply couldn't keep away even though he risked rebuke because of his act. But his father took him into his arms, held him close, and said, "My own little child." Today, after many years, he says he can still remember "the delicious sense of belonging to my father."

How are feelings of belonging generated? By doing things together. By sharing common concerns and trusting each other with responsibilities. Keeping the person rather than the gifts central when celebrating birthdays creates a sense of belonging. The child is reassured when prayers are offered on his behalf, when his opinions are valued, and when he is included in the serious and fun experiences of the family. He feels he belongs when he is included in the responsibility and work of the family.

Finally, it must be remembered that emotional and spiritual security are much more important than economic and physical security. Even a child can endure poverty, hunger, suffering, and danger to an amazing degree if he has emotional and spiritual security.

A child who has all the material things in life will starve to death emotionally and strike out against others when he is denied meaningful relationships. On the other hand, a child who goes hungry and has few material things may well mature into a noble and courageous person if he knows the security of loving relationships.

SECURITY QUIZ FOR PARENTS

Check the answer in the appropriate column: true, false, or usually.

T F U

— — — 1. I think our children feel reasonably secure.

— — — 2. We are careful in our talk of world conditions not to create feelings of fear and apprehension.

— — — 3. We seek to avoid pushing our fears on our children.

— — — 4. If we need to be gone from home when the children return from school, we are careful to let them know our whereabouts.

— — — 5. Our child may fear our marriage is on the rocks.

— — — 6. We have always been free to hug and kiss our children and tell them of our love.

— — — 7. We make it a practice to hold our children and read to them.

50

— — — 8. We have a regular routine at our house for meals, family chores, and bedtime.

FOR DISCUSSION

1. Discuss additional things which you feel build insecure or secure feelings in the child.

2. Discuss the statement "Children are insecure as long as they do not know the limits for their behavior."

3. How serious do you feel it is for a mother to hold a job away from home?

4. List and discuss things you do together as a family.

5. Do you feel many parents substitute gifts (things) for love? Why does this build insecurity?

6. The area in which I feel most insecure as a parent is. . . .

7. Has a family move created feelings of insecurity in your child?

8. Do you think you have more or less time to spend with your child than your parents or grandparents did? Why?

9. Think of three ways more quality could be put in your family times together.

3
The Need for Acceptance

Every child comes with the message that God is not yet discouraged with man. — Rabbindranath Tagore in *Stray Birds*.

* * *

If a child lives with criticism,
   He learns to condemn.
If a child lives with hostility,
   He learns to fight.
If a child lives with ridicule,
   He learns to be shy.
If a child lives with shame,
   He learns to feel guilty.
If a child lives with tolerance,
   He learns to be patient.
If a child lives with encouragement,
   He learns confidence.
If a child lives with praise,
   He learns to appreciate.
If a child lives with fairness,
   He learns justice.
If a child lives with security,
   He learns to have faith.
If a child lives with approval,
   He learns to like himself.
If a child lives with acceptance and friendship,
   He learns to find love in the world.

— Dorothy Law Nolte

CHILDREN
NEED ACCEPTANCE

IN THE introduction to his excellent Book, *Hide or Seek*, James Dobson tells of a television interview of John McKay, the great football coach at the University of Southern California. The coach was asked to comment on John, Jr., a successful player on his father's team. "I'm pleased that John had a good season last year. He does a fine job and I *am* proud of him," the coach admitted. "But I'd be just as proud if he had never played the game at all."

McKay's acceptance of his son did not depend on the son's ability or lack of it, or on his performance or lack of it.

Unfortunately, parents often convey the idea to their child that he is accepted when he succeeds but unaccepted when he fails. Acceptance provides healthy soil for growth and self-confidence. Belitting a child — or sometimes accepting him and other times depreciating him — causes a child to see himself with a mixture of respect and scorn.

A child who does not feel accepted by his parents becomes vulnerable to destructive group pressure. He fights for acceptance from others. He is likely also to feel that God hates him.

As physical health depends mainly on proper food and exercise, so emotional health depends primarily on the proper esteem we have for ourselves. This develops through acceptance and a sense of usefulness. If the atmosphere of the home includes a happy, satisfied acceptance of the child, he feels valued and can stand strong. The way a child is accepted in the early years determines to a great extent the esteem he has of himself and others when he reaches adulthood.

The parent is a kind of mirror in which the baby sees himself, influencing his perception of himself and the kind of person he is. He absorbs the emotional climate of the home, sensing very early whether he is surrounded by caring and love or by selfishness and tenseness.

Why Do Children Feel a Lack of Acceptance?

1. Constantly criticizing a child creates feelings of failure, rejection, and inadequacy. One young man, describing his growing-up years, said, "I felt I seldom, if ever, did anything right. My parents criticized me for doing things and for not doing things. I experienced continual frustration and finally developed an inner fear of attempting anything myself. If it had not been for one person who had confidence in me and trusted me with a job during my teen years, I believe I would never have had the confidence to hold a job or to make and hold to any decision of importance."

2. *Comparing a child with others conveys a lack of acceptance.* No two children are alike and to compare one with another is a great injustice. Comparing often starts early. A mother sees her neighbor's baby and compares notes. Her child must measure up. Continual comparison builds inferiority feelings which harm personality development. Inferiority feelings grow out of the great drive for superiority.

The small child feels unaccepted when his performance in sports, music, or math does not measure up to the achievements of those with superior abilities. Each of us is inferior in some things to some other persons. If we concentrate on these, we lose heart. On the other hand, each of us has some strengths, some things in which we excel. We should focus on these.

A psychologist ran a routine test as an experiment. When he handed out the test he announced that the average person could complete it in about one fifth the time it would really take. When a bell rang, indicating that the average student's time was up, some of the brightest class members became very upset with themselves, thinking that their intelligence was slipping.

A different study of students shows what other assumptions can do. Psychologists picked an average group of students, telling the teachers these students were highly intelligent. By the end of the year, because of the enthusiasm and high expectations of the teacher, their performance surpassed that of the most brilliant group in school.

3. *Expecting a child to achieve his parents' unfulfilled dreams causes him to feel unaccepted.* A father may have wanted to be a doctor. But he never made it. So from the time his son is born he plans for his son to go to medical school. Many parents, without thinking, want their child to fulfill the hopes they never realized. Imposing such expectations on a child causes him to feel unaccepted.

4. *Overprotecting a child often contributes to his feeling of unacceptance.* Parents are sometimes like the mother who said, "Son, I don't want you to get into the water until you've learned to swim." But how shall the son learn to swim? Underprotection is less dangerous than overprotection. A parent obviously should seek to protect his child from danger. Yet by overprotecting the child the spirit of adventure can be damaged, instilling a spirit of fear rather than faith. Better a broken bone than a broken spirit.

5. *Expecting too much of a child builds feelings of unacceptance.* A child can sense even the unspoken anxiousness of a parent that he be a model child. Trying too hard to attain the expected behavior can fill him with feelings of inadequacy rather than self-respect and acceptance.

This does not mean indulging the child, catering to every immature whim and demand. Unacceptable behavior needs to be limited.

Acceptance means respecting a child's feelings and his personality while letting him know that wrong behavior is unacceptable. Acceptance means that parents *like* the child all the time, regardless of his acts or ideas.

What Builds a Sense of Acceptance?

If a feeling of acceptance is so essential for self-confidence and accomplishment, what are some things every parent can do to let the child know he is accepted?

1. Recognize the child as unique. When a mother of two boys shared with her husband the happenings of the day, she found herself saying, "One of the boys did this," or "One of the boys said that." She was treating them with a sameness which robbed them of their individuality.

No two children are alike. Clyde Beatty recognized differences among animals in his training of lions. "No two lions are alike," he said. "Queenie is sullen and Brutus is playful. Nero is mean and Napoleon is moody. If you treat them all alike you're in trouble."

So also each child is different. To treat children all alike invites problems. Sometimes parents say, "I can't understand what went wrong with our youngest. We treated them all alike." That very attempt to treat them all alike may have caused the problem. To recognize different abilities, to avoid comparison of children, and to treat each child as unique gives a sense of acceptance.

61

When one child is given a gift, a parent should not encourage the idea that other children in the family should also receive a gift at the same time. Of course a parent should be concerned that over a period of time things roughly equal out. But to develop a feeling among children that cannot allow a brother or sister to receive a gift, without receiving a gift oneself, encourages selfishness.

Each child should be taught to share in the joy of another's gifts. The parent should think of each child as unique. When he sees a gift he knows would be especially appreciated by one child, he ought to be free to give it with the understanding that when he sees a gift suitable for another child at another time he will give that.

Every child should know that his parents like him just the way he is. He should feel that they like the color of his eyes, his hair, his stocky or slim build, his active or quiet manner. The more parents love the child as he is, the more accepted he will feel.

2. *Help the child find satisfaction in achievements.* One father shared how he was criticized for allowing his small son to use the garden Rototiller. His son was so small he had to reach high above his head to hold the handles. But his father walked close beside him and encouraged him.

To this boy running a Rototiller was quite an achievement. And he felt real satisfaction in doing it. A wise father stands by his child when he attempts all kinds of adventurous things. In standing by, rather than being overprotective, he is not only accepting his child, but preparing him for life.

3. *Let the child know you love him, want him, and really enjoy him.* A child is a gift from God, a heritage of the Lord. One of the most devastating things a child can experience is to feel that he was an accident, the result of an unwanted pregnancy, a forced marriage, or that he is a hindrance to the parents' happiness, or a financial burden, or a block to their enjoyment of social activities.

A child senses quickly the nature of the parent's feelings toward him. Happy is that child who is continually reminded by his parents that they want him and enjoy him to the fullest. How does a child know this? He knows it when the parent takes time to be with him, to help him with his little projects, and when the parent takes every opportunity to demonstrate love for him.

4. *Accept the child's friends.* Friends are terribly important to the child. Home should be a place where he can freely bring his friends, and a place where his friends love to come.

Many a child develops poor friendships and strained relationships because he has not felt free to bring his friends home. When parents are openly critical of their child's friends they are hurting him. Letting a child know you appreciate his friends will contribute to his own feeling of acceptance.

5. *Maintain an honest, genuine relationship with the child.* Too often parents seem to demand perfection of a child. This is harmful to the

parents and the child. When we are honest enough to confess our own failures and the fact that we as parents are not perfect, we relieve a lot of uncomfortable tension and give hope to the child. If parents could more easily admit their mistakes and even laugh at them, the atmosphere of many homes would greatly improve.

A father told how his son came home from school with a low grade in algebra. "By the time I was done with him," he said, "my son must have felt that I had always received straight As in algebra. However, what were the facts? After I had completed one semester of algebra the teacher called me in and said, 'You are so poor in algebra, I'm going to pass you just to get rid of you.' By pretending I was so superior I gave my son a feeling of hopelessness. If I had been honest and told him I know what he is going through, because I also had a rough time in algebra, I would have given my son hope."

This pretense of perfection is played out repeatedly by many parents. They imply, "I'm perfect. I never goof like you. I'm the example you ought to follow." In so doing, they frustrate the child. This attitude contributes to the child's feeling that he is not accepted.

Perhaps your child is afraid of the dark and fusses about going to bed. If you honestly say, "I know how you feel. I used to be afraid of the dark too," you will help your child overcome his fear. If you call the child a coward and tell him he ought to be ashamed of himself for being afraid, you let him know how unacceptable he really is to you. How much better it is to accept his feelings as normal and encourage him to discuss them with you. Fears talked about lose their terror.

6. *Listen to what the child is saying.* Really listening is one of the best ways of saying, "I accept you." True communication depends upon acceptance. We all share to the extent we feel we will continue to be accepted and loved. Whenever we hear someone gasp at what we've said, we immediately close up. But when someone listens, with a deep caring for us, to our good and bad, to our joys and heartaches, our successes and failures, we know that person accepts us.

A child feels accepted when the parent takes time to listen. Love, for the child, is usually spelled TIME. Let me share a letter which says it well.

Dear Folks:
Thank you for everything, but I am going to Chicago and try and start some kind of a new life.

You asked me why I did those things and why I gave you so much trouble, and the answer is easy for me to give you, but I am wondering if you will understand. Remember when I was about six or seven and I used to want you to listen to me? I remember all the nice things you gave me for Christmas and my birthday and I was really happy about the things — for about a week — but the rest of the time during the year I really didn't want presents. I just wanted all the time for you to listen to me like I was somebody who felt things too, because I remember even when I was young I felt things. But you said you were busy.

Mom, you are a wonderful cook and you had everything so clean and you were tired so much from doing all those things that made you busy. But you know something, Mom? I would have liked crackers and peanut butter just as well if you had only sat down with me a while during the day and said to me, "Tell me about it so I can maybe help you." And when Donna came I couldn't understand why everyone made so much fuss, because I didn't think it was my fault that her hair was curly and her skin so white, and she doesn't have to wear glasses with thick lenses. Her grades were better too, weren't they?

If Donna ever has children, I hope you will tell her to pay some attention to the one who doesn't smile very much because that one will really be crying inside. And when she's about to bake six dozen cookies, to make sure first that the kids don't want to tell her about a dream or something, because thoughts are important to small kids even though they don't have too many words to use when they tell about what they have inside them.

I think that all the kids who are doing so many things that grown-ups are tearing out their hair worrying about are really looking for someone that will have time to listen a few minutes and who really and truly will treat them as they would a grown-up who might be useful to them, you know — polite to them. If you folks had ever said to me, "Pardon me" when you interrupted me, I'd have dropped dead!

If anyone asks you where I am, tell them I've gone looking for someone with time, because I've got a lot of things I want to talk about.

Love to all,
Your son

7. *Treat the child as a person of worth.* A couple was complimented by neighbors for treating their children "like company." The parents were puzzled at first. Then it dawned

on them that when they said, "Please," "Thank you," "Excuse me," and in general tried to be polite, people who were not used to such things thought they were treating their children "like company."

Children are company in the sense that they should be respected as persons.

Some folks push their children out of the way instead of saying, "Excuse me" or "May I get by, please?" The way to teach the child respect is to respect the child.

John Locke years ago advised, "The sooner you treat him like a man, the sooner he will be one." Children have a remarkable ability to live up to their reputation. Call a child a rascal and he'll probably act like one. Call him bad and he's likely to prove it. Tell your friends he's a little devil and they'll soon see that he is.

On the other hand, the parent who expects his child to give him happiness and help finds a child who, though he sometimes fails, lives up to his dad's or mother's expectations.

8. *Allow the child to grow and develop in his own, unique way.* Parents have a strong tendency to exert pressure on their children — especially on the oldest child. Parents compare notes with neighbors. They take pride in the child and show off his achievements. They want their child to be different, to excel in behavior and accomplishments. They demand grownup behavior almost immediately.

Parents often have strong ideas on how the child will measure up in music, sports, intelligence, beauty, and the like. All this puts great strain on the child and can have an adverse effect on him. One mother of five grown children said, "If I had it all to do over, I'd try to allow each child to grow in a more relaxed atmosphere. I'd try to let the unique interests and qualities of each child develop more readily."

Finally, only as the child feels accepted by the parents does the child feel accepted by others and by God. Each child is as unique as his own fingerprints. Psychologist Duval suggests as a cardinal rule, "Accept the child you have and learn to enjoy him for the very special person that he is." There is so much to enjoy in each child. The time to enjoy and accept a child is during the day in his play and activities, not after he is tucked away in bed or after he is grown and gone.

ACCEPTANCE QUIZ FOR PARENTS

Check the answer in the appropriate column: true, false, or usually.

T   F   U

— — — 1. I accept my child for who he is and not for his performance.

— — — 2. I encourage my child more than I criticize him.

— — — 3. I avoid the temptation of comparing my child with others.

— — — 4. I feel that I am not overprotective.

— — — 5. I try to treat each child as a
unique individual.

— — — 6. I look into my child's eyes when
he speaks to me.

— — — 7. I treat my child as courteously as
I do company and friends.

— — — 8. I admit my mistakes and wrong
attitudes to my child.

— — — 9. I seek to avoid rebuking my child
when he expresses fear or apprehension.

— — — 10. My child feels free to bring his
friends home.

FOR DISCUSSION

1. Give additional examples of how children are pressured to fulfill their parents'
dreams.

2. Discuss the difficulty of accepting the child
himself while letting him know his behavior is
unacceptable.

3. Discuss the suggestion that a parent should
be free to give one child a gift without giving a
gift to his other children at the same time.

4. Discuss concrete ways to let a child know
you love him. Illustrate from your own experience.

5. How can a parent warmly receive his
child's friends when the parent feels those

friends are not the best company for the child?

6. Discuss the problem of a parent's temptation to pose as the "perfect parent" and what effect this may have on a child.

7. Do you feel you pushed your first child too hard?

4
The Need to
Love and Be Loved

When God wants a great work done in the world or a great wrong righted, he goes about it in a very unusual way. He doesn't stir up his earthquakes or send for his thunderbolts.

Instead he has a helpless baby born, perhaps in a simple home and of some obscure mother. And then God puts his idea into the mother's heart and she puts it into the baby's mind.

And then God waits.

The greatest forces in the world are not the earthquakes and the thunderbolts. The greatest forces in the world are babies. — E. T. Sullivan

* * *

Nature kindly warps our judgment about our children, especially when they are young, when it would be a fatal thing for them if we did not love them. — George Santayana

* * *

I love these little people; and it is not a slight thing when they, who are so fresh from God, love us. — Charles Dickens

* * *

Children do not know how their parents love them, and they never will till the grave closes over those parents, or till they have children of their own. — P. Cooke

CHILDREN NEED
TO LOVE AND BE LOVED

IN HIS BOOK *Reality Therapy*, well-known psychiatrist Dr. William Glasser states his belief that there is no such thing as mental illness. The deviant symptoms that we have come to classify as mental illness, Glasser claims, are the result of a frustration of two basic needs of life. These needs are to love and be loved. If either of these needs is not met, people tend to break emotionally. As Victor Hugo put it, "The supreme happiness of life is in the conviction that we are loved."

The tiny tot, the growing child, the teenager, the unmarried adult, the parent, and the aged — all need affection and expressions of love. And love dare not be taken for granted.

Dr. Rene Spitz, a New York psychoanalyst, spent three months observing the reaction of babies in a foundling home where the nursing staff was so busy that each child had "one tenth of a mother." Dr. Spitz found that approximately 30 percent of the babies died before they were a year old. "Emotional starvation is as dangerous as physical starvation," says Dr. Spitz. "It's slower but just as effective. Without emotional satisfaction children die."

The inner drive to love and be loved is very strong. All through life we want to make friends. As parents, the way we extend love to our child profoundly affects his ability to relate effectively to others. The degree to which we include our child in our lives, show him love, respond to his love — to that extent he is capable of including others in his life, in his friendships, and in his love.

Dr. John G. McKensie says, "There can be no question of the fact that to be loved and to love does give that sense of belonging to someone, that sense of security which is necessary for the possession of confidence. Without confidence we cannot face life."

In his sonnet "Doors," Hermann Hagedorn expresses the feeling of a child who has been unloved.

Like a young child who to his mother's door
   Runs eager for the welcoming embrace,
    And finds that door shut, and with troubled face
Calls and through sobbing calls, o'er and o'er
Calling, storms at the panel — so before
   a door that will not open, sick and numb,
   I listen for a word that will not come,
And know, at last, I may not enter more.

Silence! And through the silence and the dark
    that closed door, the distant sob of tears
Beats on my spirit, as on fairy shores
The spectral sea; and through the sobbing, hark!
    Down the fair-chambered corridor of years,
The quiet shutting, one by one, of doors.

So the unloved child meets "closed doors" all through life.

When a parent is asked if he loves his child, we expect him to answer, "Of course I love my child." Yet, we are told, the more important question is "Do your children know they are loved?"

A study of maladjusted teenagers in a large Oklahoma high school underscores how important it is to tell the child that he is loved.

First the counselors worked a long time to gain the rapport and confidence of ten students whom the faculty felt were the most neglected and maladjusted in the school. Then the team asked each of them, "How long has it been since your parents told you they loved you?" Only one of the students remembered hearing it at all, and he couldn't remember when.

In contrast, the counselors used the same procedure with ten persons the faculty felt were the best-adjusted students in the school and accepted as outstanding leaders. Without exception all of them answered that they had been assured verbally of their parents' love within the past twenty-four hours. They responded with answers such as, "This morning," "Last evening," and "Yesterday."

1. *Love is a learned response*. We learn to

love. A child is born without knowing how to love but with great capacity to love. Some babies, when denied love, literally wither away and die. Other children develop twisted personalities.

A child needs warm, outgoing affection daily. He needs the comforting arm of love when he is in trouble as much as he needs food and fresh air. In fact he needs love most when he is unlovely or in trouble.

As a baby receives love, he responds to that love and learns to give love in return. This response keeps growing. Sadly, some people, particularly men, are victims of the "taboo of tenderness." But to be strong is to be tender. To be strong is to be compassionate. To be strong is to be loving. The weak are cruel, unconcerned, and lacking in love.

2. *Love between parents affects a child's ability to love*. After I spoke on family relationships to a large group of parents, a father approached me and said, "If I understand you this evening, you said the greatest thing I can do for my child is to love his mother, Is that correct?"

"That is correct," I replied.

Knowing his parents love each other provides the child with a security, stability, and sacredness about life he can gain in no other way. A child who knows his parents love each other, who hears them expressing words of love for each other, needs little explanation of the character of God's love or the beauty of sex.

This means that love is visible. It means

faithfulness in performing little acts of love. It means special thoughtfulness and kindness, and writing love letters when away from home. It means whispering loving words about my wife or husband into the ears of my child. It means praising each other in the presence of the child.

A child needs love and wants to know about love more than anything else. If true love is not demonstrated at home, a child picks up false ideas about love from movies, novels, and magazines in our sex-ridden culture. The child needs to see genuine love modeled by his parents. A high school fellow wrote, "The thing that adds to the happiness of myself and my family is the way my father and mother love each other."

3. *Love must be spoken.* Loving involves all of life. To help make love practical and to consider its implications several specifics should be mentioned.

How is love communicated? We say we feel love. That is true. Persons can communicate love in many nonverbal ways. Holding, embracing, smiling, patting on the shoulder, and looking deeply into a loved one's eyes are examples. It is important for the child to feel and sense our love in nonverbal ways.

In my family we have a simple nonverbal code which we use to convey our love. When walking along hand-in-hand, seated at the table, or whenever the time seems right, three short squeezes of the hand signals "I love you." How easy it is, and yet how meaningful. Many times before going to sleep the children will come for a good-night kiss and reach out with three short squeezes.

The most effective way to teach love is to be a model of love. As an old playwright said, "They do not love who do not show love."

But love also requires verbal expression. Some feel words of love to their children are too personal and not to be worn on their sleeve. Usually such persons contradict themselves, not hesitating to wear words of disapproval and scolding on their sleeve. To be consistent, one would expect them to let their children guess about feelings of disappointments and disapproval also. Words of love are necessary. Is it too strong to say that love not expressed in words is not true love?

One of the common expressions in every home, particularly from children, is the question, "Do you know what?" One family I know always responds immediately with, "Yes, I know what. I love you." How beautiful! A small son in the same family was seriously ill in the hospital, unable to speak. When his parents came to his bedside they whispered quietly to him, "Do you know what?" Even though he was weak and speechless, his eyes flashed back the answer clearly.

4. *Love calls for action.* To speak words of love, yet not to do what love would dictate, is also futile. A little boy said sadly, "Daddy says he loves me. But he doesn't have any time for me."

Another small son kept asking his dad to help him build a clubhouse in the backyard. The father said he would. But each weekend he was involved in a business appointment, a golf date, some pressing homework, or a social engagement.

One day the little fellow was hit by a car and was taken to the hospital in critical condition. As the father stood by the bedside of his dying son, the last thing his son said with a smile was, "Well, Dad, I guess we'll never get to build that clubhouse."

Of course the boy didn't want the clubhouse as much as he wanted his daddy.

A father told of a compliment he received from his son who had graduated from high school and was preparing to leave for college. The boy invited his dad to go on a boat trip with him. The father wasn't anxious to shoot the rapids, carry the boat around falls, and rough it in the wilds. "Well," he explained later, "I'm not a good swimmer. It looked like a rather exhausting trip. So I said to my son, 'Get one of your buddies to go with you and I'll pay the bill for both of you.'" But his son replied, "Dad, I don't want a buddy. I want you to go with me." And that was a compliment.

5. *Love involves trust.* Rufus Mosely tells how he was reared in the backwoods of the Southern mountains. Life was rugged. Nobody had much of anything. But, inspired by his parents, he won a college scholarship. On the day he left for college his father summed up his anxieties and expectations in the words, "Son, I don't know much about the world into which you are going, but I trust you." Said Mosely, "I never forgot those words."

Myers and Myers in *Homes Build Persons* write, "When parents love children wisely, they try to help them feel that they are persons in their own right." To do this involves trust. Suspicious parents produce sneaky children.

6. *Love requires a willingness to listen.* Most parents find it hard to listen. Parents are busy with the burdens of work and are often tired. A child's chatter seems unimportant. Yet we learn much more by listening than by talking — especially from a child.

Listening carefully to the little hurts and complaints and joys of a child communicates real love. Giving the child our complete attention and looking into his eyes when speaking conveys love. Have you seen a child take his parent's face in his hands and turn it toward his own? Yet how often parents look in every other direction when the child is speaking. How often the child wants to share and the parent continues to read his paper or punishes the child for interrupting.

Certainly there is a close relationship between the parent's listening to a child's concerns when he is small and the extent to which the child will share concerns when he is in his teens. The parent who takes time to understand what his child says early in life will be able to understand his child later in life. And parents who listen to their child when he is small will have a child who listens to the parent when he is older.

7. *Love means sharing experiences.* Sharing in experiences of work and play tells the child

82

his parents love and accept him. In *Farm and Ranch* magazine a mother tells how her adolescent daughter became resentful and defiant and burst into tears at the slightest reprimand.

"Instead of punishing Betty and constantly reminding her of her age, I determined to give her large helpings of love and approval," she writes. "I stopped ordering her to do certain expected duties and asked her instead to work with me and share my duties. She had had to do the evening dishes alone and rebelliously — now we did them together, chattering as we worked.

"I made it a point to give her an affectionate hug now and then, and to praise her warmly when she deserved it. Both my husband and I laid aside our hobbies in the evenings to play games with her. . . . We gradually found our child again."

Kenneth E. Eble, in his book *A Perfect Education*, says, "Laughter, love, and learning are most closely and ideally related in play." When parents show their child how to do things, when they work and play together and create a pleasant atmosphere by sharing enjoyable times, the child learns how love acts.

A sense of unity, understanding, and communication depends upon a feeling of sharing and togetherness. When this sense of sharing is absent, a feeling of loneliness and a lack of love is present.

In family conferences over the years I've asked parents, as well as grandparents, "What good times do you recall from your childhood?'' Invariably the answers reveal that the good times remembered yet today are those which were shared together as a family. What is mentioned with delight is usually an experience, though small and seemingly insignificant at the time, which was special because it was done as a family. And each time such an experience is retold it is relived again together.

So mealtime, bedtime, leisure time, work time, playtime, and all the other times for family sharing ought to be enjoyed as much as possible because all of these provide opportunities to love and be loved.

8. *Love builds open and comfortable relationships.* A child's most important reason for wanting to be good is the love of his parents for him. When that is lost he has little motivation to be good. This underscores the importance of keeping relationships open and comfortable. Love needs to be present all the time and not conditional. Dr. David Goodman advises, ''Never say to the child, 'I will love you, if . . . !' Nor say, 'I will love you, but . . . !' Just say, 'I love you' and mean it, supporting your words with caresses and embraces and care and comfort and merriment and laughter and all that a child needs to feel absolutely assured of being loved.''

Love always looks deeper than childhood pranks, to the real person. It seeks to understand the child's search for identity. Love listens even when it hurts. The runaway child is one who feels uncomfortable in a situation where there is a lack of love.

James L. Hymes, Jr., suggests that parents should fall in love with their child every day anew just because he is the way he is. The child really lives by love, not by shelter, food, or clothing.

9. *Love recognizes persons as more important than things.* As we observed earlier, it seems difficult for many parents to learn that there is more security in love than in things. Children may receive wonderful gifts and still feel hated. Why? Because they need parents not presents.

One family left their small son with some friends while they took a trip. Upon their return they gave him a beautiful and expensive toy. He burst into tears, threw the toy to the floor, jumped on it, and broke it to pieces. The parents scolded him severely.

But it doesn't take a child psychologist to understand what had happened. These parents often left their son with friends for several days. Each time they returned with gifts. Rather than throwing their arms around their son to greet him, they held in their hands a gift. He sensed that he was being bought off.

Deep within every child's heart is the desire for love. No cold gift will ever replace this.

Parents sometimes say, "I've struggled hard all my life. I'm going to make it easier for my child." Such parents usually destroy the very outcome they desire. They want to let the child know they love him deeply. But they rob the child of their time while they work hard to provide the things they think will make the child happy. The child feels that things have become more important than persons. The good intentions of such parents cannot be doubted, but the end result is tragic.

What is love then? Love is taking time for each other. It is chatting around the table or campfire. It is a family walking and running in the woods and park. It is happiness that comes from doing extra favors for each other. Love is joining hands in some project. It is playing a game all can join in and enjoy. Love is laughing at ourselves and giving another a sense of belonging. It is talking about a common concern or praying together. Love is listening. It is any word or act which creates the feeling that I love and I am loved.

LOVE QUIZ FOR PARENTS

Check the answer in the appropriate column: true, false, or usually.

T F U

— — — 1. I told my child within the past twenty-four hours that I love him.

— — — 2. We do many things together as a family.

— — — 3. My child is free to discuss with me his experiences away from home.

— — — 4. I regularly spend time playing with my child.

— — — 5. We have a family night each week.

— — — 6. Our children know that we love each other as husband and wife.

— — — 7. Our home atmosphere is one of love.

FOR DISCUSSION

1. Discuss the wisdom of placing more emphasis on persons than on things.

2. Estimate the amount of time you spend together during waking hours as a family in a week.

3. Discuss the statement "The greatest thing I can do for my child is to love his mother."

4. What specifically do you say or do in your home to express love between you and your child?

5. Discuss the statement "Suspicious parents produce sneaky children."

6. Is your love a "conditional" love most of the time?

7. Discuss the statement "I've struggled hard all my life. I'm going to make it easier for my child."

8. If you had a whole day to spend together as a family, what would you like to do?

5
The Need for Praise

When we praise a child, we encourage him to move closer to the estimate we have of his potential. We draw to ourselves the good of everything we appreciate.

*   *   *

In praising or loving a child, we love and praise not that which is, but that which we hope for. — J. W. Goethe

*   *   *

The praises of others may be of use in teaching us not what we are, but what we ought to be. — August W. Hare

*   *   *

Words of praise, indeed, are almost as necessary to warm a child into a congenial life as acts of kindness and affection. Judicious praise is to children what the sun is to flowers. — Christian Nestell Bovee

*   *   *

Seneca tells how Cornelia presented her sons to a lady who had been displaying her jewels and asking Cornelia about hers.

"Cornelia kept her talking till her children came from school. 'And these,' said she, 'are my jewels.'"

*   *   *

I can live for two months on a good compliment. — Mark Twain

No one, great or obscure, is untouched by genuine appreciation. We have a double necessity: to be commended and to know how to commend. — Fulton Oursler

*　*　*

It is a great mistake for men to give up paying compliments, for when they give up saying what is charming, they give up thinking what is charming. — Oscar Wilde

CHILDREN
NEED PRAISE

BENJAMIN WEST described how he became a painter. One day his mother left him with his sister Sally. He found some bottles of colored ink and decided to paint Sally's portrait. In the process he messed up the kitchen. When his mother returned, she said nothing about the kitchen. Picking up the paper he was working on, she exclaimed, "Why it's Sally!" And she rewarded his effort with a kiss. West said, "My mother's kiss that day made me a painter."

William James wrote, "The deepest principle in human nature is the craving to be appreciated." All of us, in the glow of feeling we have pleased, want to do more to please. When we are told we have done well, we want to do better. Dr. George W. Crane, author and social psychologist said, "The art of praising is the beginning of the fine art of pleasing."

Failing to praise one's children is a common fault of parents. Many children seldom hear a compliment. Yet they are scolded if they fail. It is all too easy to reprimand, to condemn, and to blame children, to focus on their failures and unpleasant behavior and what they didn't do. Think of the improved conduct and sheer joy which would likely result if our words of encouragement to our children equaled or exceeded our words of criticism.

In a survey reported by the American Institute of Family Relations, mothers were asked to record the number of times they made negative and positive comments to their children. They found that they criticized ten times more than they gave a favorable comment. One conclusion of the study was that it takes four positive statements to offset the effects of one negative statement to a child.

The child who does not receive normal praise and appreciation searches for it in odd, sometimes hurtful ways. An ounce of praise can accomplish more than a ton of faultfinding. And, if one looks for it, something worthy of praise can be found in every child.

Martin Luther said, "Spare the rod and spoil the child — that is true. But beside the rod, keep an apple handy to give him when he has done well."

Every day a small girl came to school dirty. The teacher thought it looked like the same dirt day after day. Being kind and understanding, she did not want to hurt the girl's feelings or embarrass her. She knew the girl wasn't getting the right attention at home. Maybe her parents didn't care, but the teacher did.

"You have very pretty hands," the teacher told her one day. "Why don't you go to the rest room and wash them so people can see how really lovely they are?"

Delighted, the girl washed her hands and came back beaming. She held up her hands proudly for her teacher.

"Oh, they're beautiful. See what a difference a little soap and water make," she told the girl as she hugged her warmly.

Every day after that the girl came to school a bit cleaner. Eventually she was one of the neatest students in school.

Why did the youngster make such a change? Because someone complimented her. By praising the good points she improved.

Persons seldom change because we point out their faults. Nor will they love us for doing so. They will likely resent us. If we want to help others become beautiful people, we should work at it through sincere praise and encouragement. Sincere praise is the warmth and tenderness all of us need to change for the better.

If we think back, it was probably the kind words of encouragement of a parent, teacher, or friend which gave us self-confidence and the good image we have of ourselves. It was the criticism we received which causes our identity problems.

In his fine book, *Adventures in Parenthood*, W. Taliaferro Thompson shares this experience: "It was the rule at our home that before a child could go out to play on Saturday morning he had to make up his bed and clean his room. The door of the room of our eleven-year-old son was at the head of the stairs. It usually stayed open and I looked in as I passed. If he had failed to set things right, I would go in and have words with him.

"One morning as I was halfway down the stairs I realized that his room was in apple-pie order; I had seen it out of the corner of my eye, and I had taken note of it. If it had been in disarray, I should certainly have gone in and begun to condemn.

"Somewhat ashamed, I retraced my steps, went in and examined his bed carefully. It was beautifully made. I could honestly compliment him on it. 'Why,' I said, 'this would have pleased the strictest inspector in camp. It would have passed inspection at West Point. . . .'

"You have seen a half-grown dog begin to wag his whole body when you pat him or speak to him in friendly tones; my son was affected in just that way. His response was immediate and amazing. 'Daddy,' he said, 'I think I'll go over and get your mail.' It was at the end of campus. 'When I come back, I'll go and get my hair cut.' We had spoken about the state of his hair several times during the week, to no avail. 'When I get back from there I think I'll wash the car.'

"I had given him deserved praise, then for him God was in His heaven, and all was right with the world. And I had come so near going on my way without saying anything about a real achievement that took time and effort and a certain amount of skill!''[*]

Praising a child does not spoil the child. It is the child who does not receive praise for worthy work when he deserves it who will seek praise in bizarre ways. So when the gang praises him for cheating or stealing he will naturally seek to become an expert at that.

Guidelines in Giving Praise

1. Praise the child's performance, not his personality. We should praise a child for his accomplishment rather than his character. After a kind word praising a child's character, such as, "You've been a real good boy," the child often responds with bad behavior. Why? He may be fearful that he cannot live up to the goodness expected of him. The child feels he must, in some way, deny what he senses isn't true.

One family reported on a trip. For half a day of travel their small son in the back seat behaved so well in being quiet that the mother finally turned and said, "Billy, you've been a real good boy this morning." After this compliment there was no end of trouble. He emptied the ashtray on the seat. He made noise and threw things around. The reason? While he was quiet he was feeling mean toward everyone in the car, angry that he had to leave home just when he and his friends had made good plans for the week. When

---

[*]W. Taliaferro Thompson, *Adventures in Parenthood* (Richmond: John Knox Press), pp. 47, 48.

Mother said he was "good" he knew better and needed to deny what she said.

Instead of commenting on character, praise should acknowledge chores well done, thoughtful acts for others, dependability, and honesty. Parents should commend a child for trying hard to do well, even when he has not been entirely successful. Praise should point out progress.

2. *Praise what the child is responsible for rather than that which he cannot help*. For example, he cannot help it if he has beautiful hair or blue eyes. To praise the child for such things can build pride and conceit. But to praise the child for acts of kindness and generosity does not spoil the child or make him proud. He needs such approval for feelings of worth. He will respond to genuine appreciation with good behavior. The child who has the approval of others can afford to be humble. The proud or boastful child is not sure of his worth.

3. *Recognize that praise is especially needed from people who are important to a child*. Parents are the most important persons in the world to the child. The child's world is small. Parents are the center of that world. And when parents praise a child, he feels loved and secure. As one son observed, "It didn't matter what any other person said. It helped a little. But when my dad said, 'That's a good job,' my world changed."

To praise a teenager means to help him overcome timidity and develop independence. Praise develops generosity, initiative, and cooperation.

Lack of recognition causes a child to feel unneeded, unwanted, and that he is a nuisance.

This is true not only between parents and children, but in other relationships at school, work, or play. One school was plagued with an unusually high drop-out rate. Something had to be done. An insightful person suggested that the faculty should become more communicative. He proposed that they talk with students in the halls, calling students by name if possible. The school soon developed an exceptionally low drop-out rate.

4. *Praise sincerely.* The child knows when you are sincere. He cannot be fooled. Praise dare not be phony. Flattery will fall flat. Sincerity teaches the child how to accept congratulations with ease and to receive honors with humility.

5. *Praise a child for what he does on his own initiative.* To do a worthy thing without being told deserves special encouragement. Such commendation leads to still greater self-reliance and confidence.

This means that a parent should be quick to praise a loser also. In a race all but one are losers. Attitudes as well as achievements are worthy of praise. To compliment a child who has tried, yet lost, gives him courage to keep trying and motivation for the tough times every person must face.

Alta Mae Erb, in *Christian Nurture of Children*, writes, "A child may also be discouraged in self-confidence by giving him too hard a task for his ability and then trying to hold him to a high standard of accomplishment. The comments on the first cake are more important than the taste of the cake."

6. *Keep in mind that the sooner praise comes, the better.* If the parent is on hand when the success is realized, it is good. If the parent is present when a child has tried and not succeeded and then gives an encouraging word, it is even better.

7. *Remember that parents' attitudes are just as important as their words in giving encouragement.* The way a parent stops what he is doing to listen, the way a parent shares in the success or failure, the tone of a parent's voice — all these create an atmosphere which encourages or discourages the child.

If a child lives with praise, he learns to appreciate. An adult can get along without daily praise. A child cannot. He must have it to develop. He will shrivel up without praise. Fortunate is the child who receives sincere and genuine praise.

Will Sessions, discussing the topic "If I Had a Teenager," says, "I would bestow praise. If the youngster blew a horn I would try to find at least one note that sounded good to my ear, and I would say a sincere word about it. If the school theme was to my liking, I would say so, hoping that it would get a good grade when it was turned in. If his choice of shirt or tie, of socks or shoes, or any other thing met my liking, I would be vocal."

Probably no other thing encourages a child to love life, to seek accomplishments and gain confidence, more than proper, sincere praise — not flattery, but honest compliments when he does well."

PRAISE QUIZ FOR PARENTS

Check the answer in the appropriate column: true, false, or usually.

T   F   U

— — — 1. I freely compliment and praise my child.

— — — 2. When my child talks to me, I pay as much attention as when an adult talks.

— — — 3. I believe my child feels appreciated by me as a parent.

— — — 4. My child expresses appreciation for what I have done or said.

— — — 5. I praise my child for performance rather than personality.

— — — 6. I praise my child when he is loser as well as when he wins.

— — — 7. I feel that the atmosphere of our home is one which encourages.

FOR DISCUSSION

1. Record for a day or two the times you express appreciation and the times you express negative or critical comments about your child.

2. Recall examples when your child responded to praise. How did he act? What did he do?

3. Can you remember any changes that came

about in your child because of criticism?

4. Discuss the difference between destructive and constructive criticism?

5. Report on times when a word of praise or encouragement helped you gain confidence and satisfaction. Who were these friends?

6. Discuss what happens to a child if parents are upset when he loses in some sport or other effort.

7. What additional guidelines would you suggest regarding praise?

8. Discuss the statement "A child usually lives up to his reputation."

9. What is the main joy you receive in being a parent?

10. Do you think it is possible to praise a child too much?

6
The Need for Discipline

My son, do your father's bidding,
   and reject not your mother's directions . . .
for their bidding will throw light upon your life,
   their direction will enlighten you,
   and to be trained thus is the way to live.
   — Proverbs 6:20, 23, Moffatt

* * *

Children, the right thing for you to do is to obey your parents as those whom the Lord has set over you. The first commandment to contain a promise was:

   Honour thy father and thy mother
   That it may be well with thee, and that thou
      mayest live long on the earth.

Fathers, don't over-correct your children or make it difficult for them to obey the commandment. Bring them up with Christian teaching in Christian discipline. — Ephesians 6:1-4, Phillips

* * *

Parents, never drive your children to resentment or you will make them feel frustrated. — Colossians 3:21, *The Jerusalem Bible*

* * *

The beginning is the most important part of any work, especially in the case of a young and tender thing; for that is the time at which the character is being formed and the desired impression is more readily taken. Shall we just carelessly allow children to hear any casual tales which may be devised by casual persons, and to receive ideas into their minds the very opposite of those which we would wish them to have? — Plato

* * *

You can do anything with children if you only play with them. — Eduard Bismark

* * *

Beware of fatiguing them by ill-judged exactness. If virtue offers itself to the child under a melancholy and constrained aspect, while liberty and license present themselves under an agreeable form, all is lost, and your labor is in vain. — Francis de S. Fenelon

CHILDREN
NEED DISCIPLINE

A TWELVE-YEAR-OLD boy filled out a school questionnaire. In the space provided for his father's or guardian's name he wrote his father's name. The next line asked for "relationship." His son wrote "very good."

If relations are to be good between parents and children, one of the principle functions of the parent is to set limits of behavior. Effective discipline requires wisdom, patience, and persistence.

To say that love is all that is needed to be a good parent is as untrue as to say that love is all that is needed for a successful marriage. Nearly all divorced persons will admit they loved their partner at one time.

Bruno Bettelheim in *Love Is Not Enough* says that feelings of warmth, affection, and love must be tempered by knowledge, understanding, and self-control on the part of the parent. All of us know parents whose philosophy is to never say "no" to their children. Such parents rear children who care for nothing and no one. The West Coast editor of *Look*, Leonard Gross, once wrote, "A child with unlimited freedom gets frightened; he suspects he isn't loved."

A teacher bought a large fishbowl and filled it with water. When it had reached room temperature, he placed some fish in the bowl. But the fish acted strange, bunching together at the center of the bowl without much movement. A few days later, he purchased colored stones for the bowl. After he placed the stones in the bowl, the fish swam around freely. The stones in the bottom had revealed the limits of the water which the fish had not known.

In much the same way a child who does not know the boundaries for his behavior feels insecure and unloved. He finds freedom when he knows for certain where the limits are. Dr. Peter G. Crowford, child psychologist from Augusta, Georgia, says that emotional problems among the young are caused, not by firm discipline, but by lack of it. Youth need limits.

A child will not always feel warm toward a parent, no matter how hard the parent tries. The parent who requires constant approval and affection from his child is soon in trouble. A responsible parent must make some unpopular decisions. If he gives in when he knows what real love dictates for the child's good, he will, in time, lose his child's respect and his child.

Wallace Denton in his practical book, *Family Problems and What to Do About Them,* points out that effective parents usually possess certain basic qualities. "Among these are: (a) An ability to accept the child warmly. Without this the child is thwarted in being able to love healthily and perceive himself to be a worthwhile person. (b) Consistent parenting behavior. That is, the way a parent relates to the child is consistent from day to day. Some parents seem to love the child one hour and hate him the next. A child from a consistently harsh home is possibly better off than one in which the parent vacillates between love and rejection. (c) The establishment of clear limits of behavior. The particular limits may vary from family to family. It is important that they be clearly understood by the child and consistently enforced by the parent. Without limits the child becomes confused and anxious. Without learning to live within limits at home, the child will have difficulty living within the reality limits once he moves into the outside world."

1. Discipline defined. Discipline is usually defined as punishment to bring about obedience. This is far too narrow. The word "discipline" comes from the root word "disciple." And both "discipline" and "disciple" come from the Latin word for pupil, meaning to instruct, to educate, and to train. Discipline involves the total molding of the child's character through encouraging good behavior and correcting unacceptable behavior. Punishment is the part of discipline which provides a short-term, temporary deterrent.

Punishing bad behavior does not automatically produce good behavior. Discipline includes also the responsibility of the parent to draw out, encourage, and build good behavior to take the place of the bad. Discipline includes both nurture and restriction — two necessary elements for living. A good gardener nurtures and prunes his plants for good fruit. Weeds flourish naturally without special care. It is training we wish to provide for our child. Thinking of discipline in these broader terms helps us realize that methods of discipline can be more varied than we usually assume. Discipline includes everything a parent does or says to help his child learn and develop to maturity.

2. *Purposes of discipline*. Parents must continually ask themselves, "What is the ultimate goal we are working toward in the training of our children?"

3. *Methods of discipline*. The child's reaction to parental discipline is of far greater significance than the method used. Here are a number of short guiding principles you may find helpful:

Positive action usually elicts desirable behavior sooner than negative action.

Use praise more than blame.

Foresee problem areas and seek to deal with them before conflict develops.

Encourage rather than nag.

Strive for fairness.

Listen to explanations before making final conclusions.

Be consistent, but not inflexible.

110

Avoid ridicule, sarcasm, and irony.

Explain your decisions when possible, but expect instant obedience when necessary.

Set definite, clear limits of behavior, avoiding detailed or arbitrary rules that confuse.

Make absolute decisions slowly, especially when tense or tired. Use "maybe" instead of "no," or "I'll think it over."

Consider individual differences in children and make judgments accordingly.

If negative measures are warranted, administer them wisely.

Distinguish between training and punishment. Many careless and awkward actions can be improved only by consistent reminders over a long period of time, whereas deliberate misconduct should be punished immediately.

Punish on the basis of motive, not of results. A lie should be dealt with more severely than a spilled bowl of cereal.

Fit the punishment to the offense. Public humiliation or group chastening is seldom effective.

Avoid disciplinary measures at the table. A harmonious atmosphere during meals should be encouraged.

Delay severe punishment until you are calm and controlled. Impulsive decisions are usually regretted.

Do not threaten the child. Either punish or forgive him.

Do not punish the child by making him do things he should enjoy. For example, parents have sometimes forced a child to read poetry or the Bible for punishment.

Keep rules at a minimum but enforce those which are established.

Methods of discipline can be summarized under three headings: (1) regulation, (2) imitation, and (3) inspiration.

Regulation is particularly important in the

early years. Demands need to be made clear and understandable. A child will respect a parent who sets rules. A child will respect the parents' punishment when these are broken more than scoldings or threats which are not clear. An eight-year-old said, "We had a substitute teacher today. She left us do anything we wanted and we didn't like her." Children become confused and unhappy when allowed to do what they know is wrong.

At times discipline may hurt, physically and emotionally, but the parent does his child an injustice to hold off discipline because it may hurt momentarily. If a child breaks an arm, setting the bone will be painful. The child may beg the parent to prevent having it set. Does a parent consider letting the child risk being crippled to avoid the pain of the moment? Of course not. In the same way, why risk making the child a moral cripple by refusing to provide the positive training which produces good character?

Regulation means setting up rules to follow. It also assumes administering physical punishment or withholding privileges.

Although rules are important, beware of "smother love," as someone called it. To keep a youth dependent on parental regulation long after he should be making his own decisions in not wise. This can have an effect on him similar to "helping" a potential butterfly open his cocoon.

A second method of discipline is *imitation*. Walt Whitman wrote: "There was a child who went forth each day and the first object he looked upon, that object he became." A child is all ears, eyes, and open pores. He is an absorbing surface. The small child responds to persons around him and imitates them. He seeks to be like those he loves and admires. The kind of person a child becomes depends upon the kind of adults he has loved and admired. A parent should never do anything he is unwilling for his child to imitate.

A child's sense of right and wrong depends upon the emotional ties which exist between him and his parents. Careful scientific studies indicate that nondelinquents have satisfying relationships with their parents early in life while delinquents do not. If parents hope to rear disciplined children, it is imperative that first of all they set the example. An ounce of walk is worth a ton of talk. What a parent is, more than what he says, sets the model for the child.

What parents do in their own lives is far more important than what they say or the limitations they set, because the child imitates the parents in good or bad.

A cartoon pictured a puzzled father with his elbows on the dinner table. He was looking down its length at his wife and complaining, "Why can't they know that it's wrong for everybody but me to sit this way!" Someone else commented, "Children are born mimics. They behave like their parents, despite all our efforts to teach them manners."

A third method of discipline is by *inspiration*.

Here is the great secret of discipline. If parents are reasonably happy together and find fulfillment in each other, it is surprising how this overflow of contentment leads to good behavior in the children.

Discipline and control go wrong unless they exist in the framework of good feeling, affection, and fun. The actual methods of control are never as important as the parents consistency and an everpresent spirit of wanting to help the child. The child must feel the goodwill and affection of the parents. Children love and respond to smiling faces. Consistent love leads to consistent behavior. A youngster needs to know that he can always count on his parents.

The climate of the home in all its relationships has much to do with proper discipline. One mother made a bargain with her children. "I don't want to be a scolding mother," she told them. "So this week I am getting a handful of pennies. We'll divide the pennies. Anytime one of you hears me scolding, ask me for a penny. But if I find you quarreling, then you must give me a penny. Is it a deal?"

It was a deal and it helped both mother and children to build a better climate in their home.

Dobson's Five Principles of Good Discipline

One of the most helpful, practical, and down-to-earth books on discipline is James Dobson's *Dare to Discipline*. Dr. Dobson is assistant professor of pediatrics at the University of Southern California School of Medicine in Los Angeles. "I am thoroughly convinced that the proper control of children can be found in a reasonable, commonsense philosophy where five key elements are involved," he says.

The first of these principles in child discipline is to *develop respect for the parent*. This is important not for the parent's ego, but because the parent-child relationship provides the basis of all future relationships for the child.

"If you want your child to accept your values when he reaches his teen years, then you must be worthy of his respect during the younger days," Dobson advises. He notes that religion is one area where this is an important factor to consider. If the parents are not worthy of respect, then neither is their God, nor their morals.

Dobson cautions the parent to determine first whether an undesirable action represents a direct challenge of authority. Spanking youngsters of ten or less should be reserved for the moment a child expresses a defiant "I will not" or "You shut up." He says that paradoxically children want to be controlled, but they insist that their parents earn the right to control them.

The second principle Dobson recommends is to *recognize that communication often improves after punishment*. After the emotional ventilation following punishment, a child often wants to express his love by hugging the parent. The parent should respond with open arms and use the opportunity to communicate love and the reason for the punishment.

Control without nagging is the author's third

principle in child discipline. It is all too easy to tell a child to do something when both the parent and the child know that this is just a prelude to several steps which result in anger. This makes it difficult for the parent to expect instant obedience because the child knows the game, too, and is more than willing to play.

Dobson suggests as his fourth principle that parents *do not saturate the child with excessive materialism*. He feels that temporary deprivation heightens appreciation. Excessive materialism diminishes the thrill of receiving. Says Dobson, "Although it sounds paradoxical, you actually cheat the child of pleasure when you give him too much."

His fifth suggestion to parents is to *avoid extremes in control and love*. If a parent is too harsh, the child suffers the humiliation of total domination. He lives in constant fear and is unable to make his own decisions. Excessive permissiveness is equally tragic because the child is taught that the world is his own private domain and disrespects those closest to him.

Dobson also mentions another aspect of our society that has heightened the parent-child dilemma — the home in which the mother and father represent opposite extremes. The father tends to be more unsympathetic and quicker to deal out punishment. He thinks of home as a place to escape from the pressures of the workaday world. He likes to be able to rest and is short-tempered with the children who soon learn to stay out of his way. Since Mother often has no outside job, she tends to overcompensate for Dad's abruptness by going in the opposite direction with equal force. The child is caught somewhere in the middle. He respects neither parent because each one effectively undercuts the authority of the other.

Children obey and honor their parents not so much because the Bible says they should, nor because the parents do everything right. Rather, they respond to love, understanding, and meaningful relationships with their parents in their work and play and daily living together.

DISCIPLINE QUIZ FOR PARENTS

Check the answer in the appropriate column: true, false, or usually.

T   F   U

—— —— —— 1. I feel my child respects me as a person.

—— —— —— 2. I vary my discipline with different children and age levels.

—— —— —— 3. I avoid saying, "Do it because I told you so."

—— —— —— 4. I do not punish to give expression to my own anger.

—— —— —— 5. I convey my love to my child after punishment.

— — — 6. I feel we clearly understand in our family what conduct is permitted and what is not.

— — — 7. We stand together as husband and wife in the discipline of our child.

FOR DISCUSSION

1. Discuss the meaning of discipline.

2. Why does each child need discipline?

3. Do you agree with the statement "A child will kick until he feels the walls."

4. How can a parent invite misbehavior?

5. Do you find communication with your child easier after punishment?

6. Which is best, discipline without love or no discipline at all?

7. Respond to the statement "A parent can discipline a four-year-old boy by whipping him but a teenager needs counsel."

8. Are you stricter or more permissive with your child than your parents were with you?

9. If possible, read *Dare to Discipline* by James Dobson, published by Regal.

10. Take and discuss the quiz in Appendix A, "How Permissive Are You?" beginning on page 136.

7
The Need
for God

No man ever wetted clay and then left it, as if there would be bricks by chance and fortune.
— Plutarch

* * *

Religious words have value to the child only as his experience in the home gives them meaning. — Canon Lumb

* * *

Unless the Lord builds the house, those who build it labor in vain.   — Psalm 127:1

* * *

Dear Lord, I do not ask
That Thou shouldst give me some high work of
   Thine,
Some noble calling, or some wondrous task.
Give me a little hand to hold in mine.
Give me a little child to point the way
Over the strange, sweet path that leads to Thee.
Give me a little voice to reach to pray;
Give me two shining eyes Thy face to see.
The only crown I ask, dear Lord, to wear
Is this, that I may teach a little child.
I do not ask that I may ever stand
Among the wise, the worthy, or the great.
I only ask that softly hand-in-hand,
A child and I may enter at the gate.
— Author Unknown

They are idols of hearts and of households;
    They are angels of God in disguise;
The sunlight still sleeps in their tresses,
    His glory still gleams in their eyes;
These truants from home and from heaven,
    They have made me more manly and mild;
And I know now how Jesus could liken
    The kingdom of God to a child.
                — Charles M. Dickinson in *The Children*

CHILDREN
NEED GOD

WHEN PRINCESS Margaret was five years old,
the newspapers reported she came out of church
one day bitterly disappointed. The minister's
prayer disturbed her.

"Why did he only pray for you and Daddy
and Elizabeth?" she asked her mother. "I'm
just as bad as you are."

It is easy for adults to overlook the spiritual
needs and worries of children. It is important
for a child to know how he stands with God.
And it is essential that correct concepts of God
be nourished early. For example, harmful life-
long views are learned by such statements as
"God does not love you when you are naughty"
or "If you keep on being very good, you will go
to heaven." A child can never be sure of his
spiritual status when "if" statements are used.

Horace Bushnell said, "Home and religion

are kindred words, home because it is the seat of religion; religion because it is the sacred element of home. . . . A house without a roof could scarcely be a more indifferent home than a family without religion."

The Bible and the Child

A surprisingly small amount of space is given in Scripture to the subject of children. In light of the abundance of material on child-parent relationships today, we would expect the Bible to say much more on the subject. The Scriptures admonish parents to be the right kind of persons. It assumes that, if this is true, children will grow up to love God and serve Him.

One of the earliest statements of guidance for parents appears in Deuteronomy 6:6-8:

And these words which I command you this day
    shall be upon your heart;
and you shall teach them diligently to your children,
and shall talk of them
    when you sit in your house,
    and when you walk by the way,
    and when you lie down,
    and when you rise up.
And you shalt bind them as a sign upon your hand,
And they shall be as frontlets between your eyes.
And you shalt write them
    on the doorposts of your house
    and on your gates.

A number of important principles are clearly laid down here which reappear in one way or another throughout Scripture.

1. The Bible teaches that, first of all, par-

124

ents should be right with God themselves. God said of Abraham, "For I know him, that he will command his children . . . *after* him." A parent cannot long simply tell his child the way to go. If his influence is to count, he must be everything he expects his child to be. A parent must not only *know* the way and *show* the way. He must also *go* the way.

Parents who only tell their children religious facts and send them to church can have little hope of the children choosing to accept those facts or to continue going to church. "Whatever parent gives his children good instructions and sets them at the same time a bad example, may be considered as bringing them food in one hand and poison in the other," says John Balguy.

Children can understand God, love, mercy, forgiveness, acceptance, and the truth of God's Word only to the extent that they experience them in relationships, particularly in the home.

2. *The Bible puts the responsibility for the religious training of children squarely on the parents*. God ordained the home as the institution to train children in the way they should go. God didn't expect the church, the preacher, the school, or any other agency to do this. Parents dare not blame such agencies when their children go wrong.

The Deuteronomy passage quoted above says that parents shall teach diligently. The phrase used here is the same one used in Hebrew regarding surgery. Parents are to apply the truth as a surgeon applies the knife — precisely where the need exists in the life of the child.

Spiritual development begins in the home. No matter how carefully the church works with children, unless there is cooperation and encouragement in the home, the whole effort is undermined.

Richard Baxter, a famous English preacher, accepted a wealthy and sophisticated parish. For three years he preached passionately without any visible results. "Finally one day," he wrote, "I threw myself across the floor of my study and cried out, 'God, you must do something with these people or I'll die.'" And, he continued, "It was as if God spoke to me audibly and said, 'Baxter, you're working in the wrong place. You expect revival to come through the church. Try the home.'"

Baxter went from home to home leading parents to give themselves to God and setting up family worship. The fire began to burn until the entire congregation was alive and the flames of spiritual renewal spread across the land.

God places tremendous responsibility on parents to teach. This is clear in the Deuteronomy passage. Note also the following clear passage.

Responsibility to Teach
Listen to this Law, my people,
pay attention to what I say;
I am going to speak to you in parable
and expound the mysteries of our past.

What we have heard and known for ourselves,

and what our ancesters have told us,
must not be withheld from their descendants,
but be handed on by us to the next generation.

that is: the titles of Yahweh, his power
and the miracles he has done.
When he issued the decrees for Jacob
And instituted a Law in Israel,

he gave our ancestors strict orders
to teach it to their children;
the next generation was to learn it,
the children still to be born,

and these in their turn were to tell their own children
so that they too would put their confidence in God,
never forgetting God's achievements,
and always keeping his commandments,

and not becoming, like their ancestors,
a stubborn and unruly generation,
a generation with no sincerity of heart,
in spirit unfaithful to God.
— Psalm 78:1-8, *The Jerusalem Bible*

Notice how the responsibility is clearly placed on parents. The purpose for this instruction is also clear — (1) so the children also will put their faith in God, (2) so they will not forget God's act or the keeping of His commands, and (3) so they will not become unruly, stubborn, or rebellious.

Notice also the influence of faithful parents of more than one generation on the young preacher, Timothy. The Apostle Paul wrote, "I often think of that genuine faith of yours — a faith that first appeared in your grandmother Lois, then in Eunice your mother, and is now, I am

127

convinced, in you as well" (2 Timothy 1:5; Phillips).

"Yet you must go on steadily in those things that you have learned and which you know are true. Remember from what sort of people your knowledge has come, and how from early childhood your mind has been familiar with the holy scriptures, which can open the mind to the salvation which comes through believing in Christ Jesus. All scripture is inspired by God and is useful for teaching the faith and correcting error, for re-setting the direction of a man's life and training him in good living" (2 Timothy 3:14-16, Phillips).

3. *The Bible clearly teaches that the parent's instruction should be constant and continuous.* Religious instruction is to be going on by word and example all the time. It is not a hit and miss activity but should be carried out morning, noon, and night.

Many young people react negatively to a piety which is practiced only on Sunday morning or at family worship. They sense quickly the inconsistency of such a life. In his book *A Small Town Boy* Rufus Jones tells about morning worship in the home in which he grew up. "But there was something more to our family religion than this morning devotion together. The life in our home was saturated with the reality and the practice of love. . . . It was an old-fashioned home where nurture went on all the time. It was a life-building center. It was here that my anchors were forged."

God gives the child a special sensitivity to His presence and His handiwork in creation. The child grows spiritually when parents associate God with life around him. God has also filled the child with questions. We are told the average child asks 500,000 questions by the age of fifteen. That's half a million opportunities to teach. Many of these are "why" and "how" questions which take us right to the feet of God.

To many parents, freedom of religion means freedom from religion. They spend their time accumulating wealth instead of building character. Some have accepted the fallacy that they should not teach religion to the child, lest the child be prejudiced. Let the child choose, they say. But such an approach already prejudices the child. The absence of teaching about God leaves the child a prey of all kinds of false gods and philosophies.

4. *The Bible says, "Train up a child in the way he should go, and when he is old he will not depart from it."* It is true that guidance is given through instructing a child or imparting knowledge. But far the largest part of guidance is communicated through example. The word "train" refers primarily to example. The most significant religious experiences of a family consist of the things that go on between family members at home day by day.

In an article in *The Christian Home*, Donald Stuart Williamson writes, "God loves and heals persons through other persons, in the intimacy of personal relationships. That's why feelings

129

and emotional attitudes in a family are the essence of that family's religious experience." The example of parents will always follow and influence a child.

Ian Maclaren's classic book, *Beside the Bonnie Briar Bush*, includes a moving chapter called "His Mother's Sermon." It tells of a young Scottish minister, just graduated from Edinburgh, who moved with four cartloads of furniture to his first parish in Drumtockty. His maiden aunt was his housekeeper. He carefully prepared his first sermon for the new parish. It was a scholarly manuscript.

While speaking of his sermon to his aunt on Friday evening, their minds went back some five years. They recalled kneeling by the bedside of his dying mother. They remembered how she gave her son words of counsel and a testimony of faith and hope. She handed him her watch and chain and said, "There hasn't been an hour when I failed to pray for you. If God calls you to the ministry, you'll not refuse, and the first day you preach in your church, speak a good word for Jesus Christ."

His aunt reminded him of his mother's last words. These words transformed his sermon that night until his effort on the Sabbath could rightly be called his mother's sermon.

A young man expressed his preference for a particular version of the Bible. A friend replied, "I prefer my mother's translation. She has translated the Bible into the language of daily life. My mother's is the clearest translation."

Gypsy Smith wrote, "Father is getting old. Soon I'll receive word that my father has died. I'll go and look in my father's face the last time and I'll say, 'Father, you made it hard for me. You made it hard for me to go wrong!'"

Although the influence of the parent is great, we should not fall into the trap of thinking if the parent does everything perfect the child will in the end turn out right. Many times in family conferences and retreats parents ask, "Doesn't the Bible say that if we train up a child in the way he should go he will not depart from it, and even if he does depart for a time, he will return?"

The answer is that we dare not accept a determinism which takes away the choice of the child. God, our heavenly Father, does all things perfectly. He makes no mistakes, but He does not rob His created beings of the power of choice. Even those who experience His best blessings may, and sometimes do, turn from His way. Yet the promise concerning the influence and example of a godly home is a strong one.

Three Parables

In conclusion, I would like to share three parables included by Alta Mae Erb in her book *Christian Nurture of Children*:

I took a little child's hand in mine. He and I were to walk together for a while. I was to lead him to the Father. It was a task that overcame me, so awful was the responsibility.

And I talked to the little child only of the Father. I painted the sternness of the Father's face, were the child to displease Him. We walked under tall trees. I said the Father had power to send them crashing down, struck by His thunderbolt. We walked in the sunshine. I told him of the greatness of the Father who made the burning, blazing sun.

And one twilight we met the Father. The child hid behind me; he was afraid; he would not look up at the face so loving. He remembered my picture; He would not put his hand in the Father's hand. I was between the child and the Father. I wondered. I had been so conscientious, so serious.

° ° °

I took a little child's hand in mine. I was to lead him to the Father. I felt burdened by the multitude of things I was to teach him. We did not ramble. We hastened on from spot to spot. At one moment we compared the leaves of the trees, in the next we were examining a bird's nest. While the child was questioning me about it, I hurried him away to chase a butterfly. Did he chance to fall asleep I wakened him, lest he should miss something. I wished him to see. We spoke of the Father often and rapidly. I poured into his ears all the stories he ought to know but we were interrupted often by the wind blowing, of which we must speak; by the coming out of the stars, which we must needs study; by the gurgling brook, which we must trace to its source.

And then in the twilight we met the Father.

The child merely glanced at Him. The Father stretched out His hand but the child was not interested enough to take it. Feverish spots burned on his cheeks. He dropped exhausted to the ground and fell asleep; again I was between the child and the Father. I wondered. I had taught him so many, many things.

° ° °

I took a little child's hand in mine to lead him to the Father. My heart was full of gratitude for the glad privilege. We walked slowly. I suited my steps to the short steps of the child. We spoke of the things the child noticed.

Sometimes it was one of the Father's birds; we watched it build a nest, and we saw the eggs that were laid. We wondered later at the care it gave its young.

Sometimes we picked the Father's flowers, and stroked their soft petals, and loved their bright colors. Often we told stories of the Father. I told them to the child and the child told them to me. We told them, the child and I, over and over again. Sometimes we stopped to rest leaning against the Father's trees, and letting His air cool our brows, and never speaking.

And then in the twilight we met the Father. The child's eyes shone. He looked up lovingly, trustingly, eagerly, into the Father's face; he put his hand into the Father's hand. I was for the moment forgotten. I was content.

GOD QUIZ FOR PARENTS

Check the answer in the appropriate column: true, false, or usually.

T   F   U

— — — 1. I have regular times of personal prayer and Bible reading.

— — — 2. In our family, the father takes primary responsibility for spiritual leadership

— — — 3. We read the Bible and pray together regularly as a family.

— — — 4. I seek to be an example in the things I teach my child.

— — — 5. We do not "send" our children to church. We go regularly as a family.

— — — 6. Talking about God, prayer, the Bible, and religious subjects is normal in our home.

— — — 7. Our children sense that religious concerns have top priority in our home and in our decisions.

FOR DISCUSSION

1. How can Deuteronomy 6:6-8 be carried out today.

2. Discuss Canon Lumb's statement "Religious words have value to the child only as his experience in the home gives them meaning."

3. Is there value in sending a child to church if the parents do not go?

4. What does it say to a child if only the mother prays in the home or reads the children Bible lessons? What does it say about the church when only the mother and children attend?

5. Discuss the idea that the father should assume primary responsibility for spiritual things in the home.

6. How do you feel about determinism as it was raised in the latter part of the chapter?

7. Share your thoughts on the statement "A child cannot be a whole person if only the physical, social, mental, and emotional needs are met while the religious is ignored or left to develop on its own."

8. Discuss the idea that the father provides a child's first concept of God. What can be done for children who do not have a loving, kind, and considerate father?

9. Ponder the three parables at the end of the chapter and analyze why the teachers in the first two failed and why the third approach succeeded.

APPENDIX A

HOW PERMISSIVE ARE YOU?

A quiz to help parents find the middle ground between too much and too little freedom for their children.

Permissiveness has become a fighting word among parents and the child psychologists. The prevailing wisdom now holds that it is possible to give a child too much freedom. But on the other hand, the youngster of today has shown that he simply will not accept many of the restraints his parents did when they were young.

All this leaves many fathers and mothers in a quandary. "Parents often feel they're walking a tightrope between being permissive and being tyrannical," says W. T. Byers, noted child psychologist. "Common sense tells them to be a little of both, but they're bothered by doubts about when to be one or the other."

To help clear away these doubts, and to give parents some idea of exactly how permissive they are, Byers and other child psychologists have developed the quiz that follows. Check your answers against the experts, and then decide how much permissiveness is too much.

Questions

1. Should boys and girls under 12 be required to help with chores like washing dishes, making beds, and dusting? Yes. No.

2. Your neighbor complains that your son has trampled her flower bed. Would you: (a) decide it was a lot of fuss over nothing; (b) punish the child;

(c) scold the youngster and make him apologize?

3. Your child wants a new bike which you can't really afford. Do you: (a) tell him he can't have it; (b) find the money for it; (c) promise the bike later when finances permit?

4. Your child insists on watching a TV show you consider too violent. Would you: (a) let him watch it anyway; (b) turn to a different show; (c) turn the set off?

5. When your youngsters are not at home, are you reasonably sure where they are? Yes. No.

6. In deciding how much allowance your child gets, do you base the amount on: (a) how much you earn; (b) how much your child's friends get; (c) how much you think is best for your child?

7. Should you, as a punishment, send a child under 12 to bed without dinner? Yes. No.

8. Your child complains that his homework is too difficult. Should you: (a) sit down and help him with it; (b) tell him to struggle with it some more; (c) call his teacher the next day to find out what's wrong?

9. To encourage your child to do well on exams, you should: (a) warn him he better do well, or no more TV watching; (b) promise him a reward if he does well; (c) keep calm and explain that the results of the exam are up to him.

10. Do you still read to your children, even though they can read well enough themselves? Yes. No.

Answers

1. Yes. In a recent Los Angeles survey, only 28 percent of the parents questioned said they insisted that boys and girls perform regular household chores. Some permissive mothers and fathers explained that since the chores usually weren't done

right, it was hardly worth the trouble insisting the children do them. Others simply said it wasn't necessary for youngsters to help. Says psychologist Byers: "By not demanding regular chores from their children, parents fail to train them for life, where each person has to carry his own weight. Many parents don't realize where loving care ends and spoiling begins."

2. c. Byers posed this question to 200 parents. Nearly half answered that the neighbor was making too much fuss. Only 30 said they would scold the youngster and send him to the neighbor to apologize. "Regardless of what a parent may think of a certain individual," comments the psychologist, "a child should never be encouraged to neglect his social obligation to that person."

3. a. In Byers' survey, 80 of 200 said they would try to find the money to buy the youngster a bike. Most of the others answered they would try to buy something less expensive. "Having the courage to say no," says the psychologist, "has become a rare parental virtue these days."

4. b. "The important issue here," comments Byers, "is not only whether TV violence might harm a child, but whether the parent explicitly expresses approval or disapproval of the program. A consistently strict parent who might turn out to be wrong on some issues exerts less harm on a child's upbringing than a permissive parent who agonizes over whether he's doing the right thing. Turning the set off should be only a last resort."

5. Yes. Young children according to Byers, feel more secure and are less likely to get into trouble when their parents know where they are and who they are with.

6. c. "A parent cannot rely on how much money other children receive in determining the amount of

his own youngster's allowance," says Byers. "Nor can he base that sum on how much he earns, unless he is in dire financial straits. The only concern should be what the parent thinks is truly the proper amount for his youngster."

7. Yes. "Sending a child to bed without any dinner is more effective than a spanking," says Dr. Wolfgang Lederer. "If this form of punishment is administered only occasionally, parents needn't worry about their youngster starving."

8. b. Doing too much for a child can cause more harm than not doing enough," says Lederer. Parents who develop the habit of helping with homework create a dependency reaction that lets the child pay less attention to classwork.

9. c. I believe it is the atmosphere we build up in the home which encourages a child's effort, not bribery or threats," says educational pyschologist Philip J. Oliver.

10. Yes. Oliver comments: "Reading aloud to one another is one of the best means of communication between adults. A parent who introduces his child to this pastime is treating the youngster to one of life's greatest joys, as well as cultivating a healthy desire for intellectual self-improvement."

APPENDIX B

Understanding Age Growth

This chart seeks to summarize some of the characteristics which the majority of youth experience. Resources for this material include the Minnesota Department of Health, as well as the writings of Dr. Arnold Gesell, Dr. Kent Gelbert, Dr. Frances L. Ilg, Dr. Milton I. Levine,

John Leuellen, and Willard C. Olson. Reprinted by permission from *Sex Education,* Approach/Program/Resources/For the parish. Copyright 1968. Sacred Design Associates, Inc., 840 Colorado Avenue, So., Minneapolis, Minnesota 55416.

	PHYSICAL	SOCIAL	SPIRITUAL	SEXUAL
AGE 5 Kindergarten	Child can run, jump, climb. Learns to hop and skip this year. Child grows approximately 6 inches and gains about 10 pounds in weight. Can dress self, tie shoes, brush teeth, button clothes. Gains reading readiness.	Children learn to relate to others outside the home. Activity with others is very important at this age. Children should learn give and take in preparation for life. The child likes to be at home with mother, or to know she is near.	Accepts fact of God as Creator and loving Father. Sometimes confuses names and persons of God and Jesus. At times worries over ideas that God sees everything he does. Likes stories from the Bible. Usually enjoys being in the church school class.	Child is usually curious about "where he came from." Asks many questions about babies. Is curious about the difference between male and female. Family unit is good beginning for basic sex information, which should be gradually progressive at each succeeding age.

	Physical	Social	Spiritual	Family/Sex
AGE 6 Grade 1	Child continues high energy. Coordination improves. Begins to lose front baby teeth. Difficult to sit still for long periods of time. Attention span short. Learns to read and gets numbers concept.	Social adjustment must be made at this age. Child learns to interact with others in higher grades. He gradually learns how to control his emotions and behavior. Looks to adults for approval of actions.	Just beginning to develop a sense of values. God is important. He can accept the fact that God sees him, but the opposite is not true. He expects his prayers to be answered in a literal way, and immediately! He is ready for more Bible stories, the activity of dramatization. His ideas are concrete, not at all abstract as yet.	Concept of family as basic unit is of continued importance. Child is interested in new members in their family, sex differences, how they arrived, etc., as was true in kindergarten. Child is interested in "how" of reproduction. Asks questions about animal mating.
AGE 7 Grade 2	Child continues high energy. Coordination improves still more so now can handle writing and drawing tools, etc. Still has short attention span. Child is usually noisy, active. Growth is slow.	Child at this age needs help in becoming self-confident member of society. Often is dreamy and extremely sensitive to approval or disapproval of others. Child likes competition in group play,	Thinks carefully about God and heaven. Is able to participate in class discussions using more abstract concepts. The Bible heroes seem very much alive to him. He enjoys stories from the	Child of seven begins to grow more firmly from egocentricity to being a member of the community with accompanying notice of sex differences. Frequently handling of sex organs may be noted.

	but always wants to win, is a poor loser.	Bible. Is able to begin making decisions for his life's actions.	Children might disappear into the bathroom to laugh about toilet functions; they may touch each other on buttocks or genitals.
AGE 8 Grade 3 Coordination such that they can skate, do simple folk dances, etc. Grows quite a bit this year. Attention span increases so can work for longer periods.	Boys learn it is important to be brave in any situation. The child wants to appear grown up and yet depends on parents and teachers. He is inclined to be bossy. Clubs are usually of one sex. Beginning to be aware of self as a person.	His world is expanding and the mission interest can be introduced. He has many questions about things which were previously accepted on faith. Can read for himself now, from his own Bible. He can accept forgiving love in class experiences.	Modesty becomes very important to the child. Sexual questions becomes less frequent. A change in the sex glands occurs at this time; growth hormones become more active while sex hormones quiet down. Boys interested in "dirty" jokes and vulgar words. May ask about father's part in reproduction.
AGE 9 Grade 4 Growth is slowing down for boys and there is	Clubs and group activities important. Each club	This age child can grasp the history of the Bible. He	Period of getting ready for adolescence from now

	Physical	Social	Religious	Sexual
	usually a growth spurt in girls. Coordination is excellent. Some girls have the appearance of breasts and pubic hair, though most still not developing.	stays with own sex. These groups help form good behavior patterns. Enthusiasm runs faster than his abilities. Wants to be like his peers.	looks up to heroes and can be motivated greatly to Christian character and action by teachers who know and understand him. He can understand service to others and can also comprehend the idea of the worldwide church.	until thirteen years of age. Sexual development not very marked. Girls might start menstruation. Discussion of sex with friends may occur.
AGE 10 Grade 5	Girls begin to pass the boys in height. Team games more important now.	Boys and girls seem to dislike each other during fifth and sixth grades. Their humor is funny only to their peers, it seems. Girls have best friends, often several. Relationships are more involved than previously.	At this age the child is responsive and able to discuss his Christian faith. He can continue learning the facts of the Bible and apply them in his own life. He is able to find meaning in Christian stewardship.	Majority have learned about menstruation. Some interested in details of reproduction. (Girls.) Some have experienced normal sex play. Have heard of intercourse, interested in "dirty" jokes. May experience a spurt of curiosity about sex.
AGE 11 Grade 6	Competitive spirit is strong. Team sports are	Interest in Scouting and similar activities at its	The eleven-year-old begins to think of his life	Most girls know about reproduction and inter-

AGES 12, 13, 14 Grades 7, 8, 9			

AGES 12, 13, 14 / Grades 7, 8, 9

Girls maturing more quickly than boys. Boys mature about the ninth grade usually. Some seventh grade boys have pubic hair and growth of genitalia. Girls read romance stories and dream, whereas boys are more interested in sports and physical activities. Girls' breasts very popular. Quite a difference this year in physical development of girls, most have begun to show breast development and most have reached 90 percent of mature stature. Boys still don't show sexual maturation.

Boys still interested in gang or group activities. They enjoy sports and hunting with other boys. Both sexes are trying to break ties with parents. Eighth and ninth graders more interested in opposite sex to some extent. height now. Still has a strong family attachment, though seems to disparage family in conversation. Still has friends of same sex and relationships more emotional and complicated.

The junior high youth is beginning to master abstract thinking so can be led into ethical discussions. He begins to wonder and to ask questions about religion. This experience should be encouraged and should be guided by a sympathetic and able teacher. occupation and can be encouraged to relate his faith to this choice. He will respond to group activities at the church and enjoy them. He is able to create tangible expressions of his faith and should have opportunity for these creative activies.

Sex education should be honest and should have reached completion factually. Build now on strong relational aspect. Boys may experience emission of semen during sleep. Most girls will be menstruating. Teenagers wonder how to use their sexual capacities; course, though on a factual basis, biological rather than relational concept. Most boys know about masturbation and have had some experience with it. Some have erections from non-erotic stimuli.

begin to fill out, under-arm hair develops, men-arche tends to occur. Awkwardness common.

they joke about it and try petting on dates.

They sometimes think of Christ as a courageous hero who was brave to die on the cross. They need guidance in applying it personally to their own lives.

Need for adult guidance in sex education extremely important at this age. Strong sex feeling and urges are felt.

AGES 15, 16, 17, 18
Grades 10, 11, 12

Most of these youth have reached sexual maturity. Boys are extremely well coordinated in sports activities. Girls become more visibly feminine. It is important to watch for good diet in order to be strong and have good complexion. Acne is a problem.

Although it is wisest to "play the field" at this age, youth are inclined to "go steady." They find security in a regular and steady date for school affairs. They find their activities outside the home for the most part.

The youth of this age has an expanding horizon and wants to structure his own activites. An understanding leader is invaluable. This age youth is capable of deeper abstract thinking. He needs help in understanding the problem of ethics. His life is before him and the subject of Christian vocations is timely. He is capable of deep emotional response

to worship and Christian leadership. The church can take advantage of this situation.

BIBLIOGRAPHY

Ames, Louise B. *Child Care and Development*. Philadelphia: Lippincott, 1970.

Amsturtz, H. Clair. *Growing Up to Love*. Scottdale, Pa.: Herald Press, 1966.

Baruch, Dorothy. *How to Discipline Your Children*. Public Affairs Pamphlet No. 154, 381 Park Avenue, South, New York, N.Y.

Bettelheim, Bruno. *Love Is Not Enough*. New York: The Free Press, 1950.

Briggs, Dorothy C. *Your Child's Self-Esteem: The Key to His Life*. Garden City, N.Y.: Doubleday, 1970.

Cattell, Psyche. *Raising Children with Love and Limits*. Chicago: Nelson-Hall, 1972.

Cheavens, Frank. *Creative Parenthood: Advantages You Can Give Your Child*. Waco: Word Books, 1971.

Clinebell, Howard, and Clinebell, Charlotte. *Crisis and Growth: Helping Your Troubled Child*. Philadelphia: Fortress Press, 1971.

Craig, Sidney D. *Raising Your Child, Not by Force but by Love*. Philadelphia: Westminster Press, 1973.

Cutts, Norma E., and Moseley, Nicholas. *Better Home Discipline*. New York: Appleton-Century-Crofts, 1951.

Denton, Wallace. *Family Problems and What to Do About Them*. Philadelphia: Westminster Press, 1971.

Dobson, James. *Hide or Seek*. Old Tappan, N.J.: Revell, 1974.

——————. *Dare to Discipline*. Glendale, Calif.: Regal, 1972.

Dodson, Fitzhugh. *How to Parent*. Plainview, N.Y.: Nash Publishing, 1970.

Dreikurs, Rudolf. *Challenge of Parenthood*. New York: Hawthorne, 1948.

147

Drescher, John M. *Now Is the Time to Love*. Scottdale, Pa.: Herald Press, 1970.

Duvall, Evelyn M. *Faith in Families*. Nashville: Abingdon, 1972.

——————. *Evelyn Duvall's Handbook for Parents*. Nashville: Broadman, 1974.

Erb, Alta Mae. *Christian Nurture of Children*. Scottdale, Pa.: Herald Press, 1955.

Fremon, Suzanne S. *Children and Their Parents: Toward Maturity*. New York: Harper and Row.

Ginott, Haim. *Between Parent and Child*. New York: Avon, 1973.

——————. *Between Parent and Teenager*. New York: Avon, 1973.

Glover, Leland E. *How to Give Your Child a Good Start in Life*. New York: Macmillan, 1972.

Goodman, David. *A Parent's Guide to the Emotional Needs of Children*. New York: Hawthorne Books, 1959.

Heynen, Ralph. *The Secret of Christian Family Living*. Grand Rapids: Baker, 1969.

Jacobsen, Marion L. *How to Keep Your Family Together . . . and Still Have Fun*. Grand Rapids: Zondervan, 1973.

LeMasters, E. E. *Parents in Modern America*. Homewood, Ill.: Dorsey, 1957.

Madsen, Clifford K. and Charles H. Madsen, Jr., *Parents, Children*. Boston: Allyn & Bacon, 1970.

Narramore, Bruce S. *Help! I'm a Parent*. Grand Rapids: Zondervan, 1975.

Narramore, Clyde M. *How to Help Your Child Develop Faith in God*. Grand Rapids: Zondervan.

——————. *Young Children and Their Problems*. Grand Rapids: Zondervan, 1961.

Peairs, Lillian, and Peairs, Richard H. *What Every Child Needs*. New York: Harper and Row, 1974.

Petersen, J. Allan. *The Marriage Affair*. Wheaton: Tyndale House.

Thompson, W. Taliaferro. *Adventures in Parenthood*. Richmond: John Knox.

Werner, Hazen G. *Look at the Family Now*. Nashville: Abingdon, 1970.

Wickes, Frances. *The Inner World of Childhood*. New York: Appleton-Century.

Winter, Gibson. *Love and Conflict: New Patterns in Family Life*. Garden City, N.Y.: Doubleday, 1958.

Young, Leontine. *Life Among the Giants*. New York: McGraw-Hill, 1965.

John M. Drescher is pastor of the Scottdale
Mennonite Church, Scottdale, Pennsylvania.
From 1962 to 1973 he edited *Gospel Herald*,
the official weekly magazine of the Mennonite
Church. He served on the board of Associated
Church Press.

Drescher's articles have appeared in approximately one hundred magazines and journals.
Much of his writing has been in the area of
family. He is the author of *Meditations for the
Newly Married, Now Is the Time to Love,
Follow Me, Heartbeats, Spirit Fruit,* and a
series of eleven Visitation Pamphlets.

John and his wife, Betty, have held numerous family and married couples retreats throughout North America. He served on the planning committee of the Continental Congress on the Family held in St. Louis in October 1975.

The Dreschers are parents of three boys and two girls: Ronald, Sandra, Rose, Joseph, and David. Family hobbies include music, crafts, camping, clocks and gardening.